PENGUIN BOOKS

THE DAY THE WORLD ENDED AT LITTLE BIGHORN

Joseph M. Marshall III, an acclaimed historian and storyteller, is the author of six previous books, including *The Journey of Crazy Horse: A Lakota History* and *The Lakota Way: Stories and Lessons for Living*, which was a finalist for the PEN Center USA West Award in 2002. Marshall was an actor in and consultant and narrator for TNT's award-winning 2005 miniseries *Into the West*. A recipient of the Wyoming Humanities Award, Marshall was raised on the Rosebud Sioux Indian Reservation and his first language is Lakota. He now makes his home in New Mexico.

Visit www.thunderdreamers.com.

JOSEPH M. MARSHALL III

The Day the World Ended
at Little Bighorn

A Lakota History

PENGUIN BOOKS

PENGUIN BOOKS
Published by the Penguin Group
Penguin Group (USA) Inc., 375 Hudson Street, New York, New York 10014, U.S.A.
Penguin Group (Canada), 90 Eglinton Avenue East, Suite 700, Toronto,
Ontario, Canada M4P 2Y3 (a division of Pearson Penguin Canada Inc.)
Penguin Books Ltd, 80 Strand, London WC2R 0RL, England
Penguin Ireland, 25 St Stephen's Green, Dublin 2, Ireland (a division of Penguin Books Ltd)
Penguin Group (Australia), 250 Camberwell Road, Camberwell,
Victoria 3124, Australia (a division of Pearson Australia Group Pty Ltd)
Penguin Books India Pvt Ltd, 11 Community Centre,
Panchsheel Park, New Delhi – 110 017, India
Penguin Group (NZ), 67 Apollo Drive, Rosedale, North Shore 0632,
New Zealand (a division of Pearson New Zealand Ltd)
Penguin Books (South Africa) (Pty) Ltd, 24 Sturdee Avenue,
Rosebank, Johannesburg 2196, South Africa

Penguin Books Ltd, Registered Offices:
80 Strand, London WC2R 0RL, England

First published in the United States of America by Viking Penguin,
a member of Penguin Group (USA) Inc. 2007
Published in Penguin Books 2008

THE LIBRARY OF CONGRESS HAS CATALOGED
THE HARDCOVER EDITION AS FOLLOWS:
Marshall, Joseph, 1945–
The day the world ended at Little Bighorn / Joseph M. Marshall III
p.   cm.
Includes bibliographical references and index.
ISBN 978-0-670-03853-4 (hc.)
ISBN 978-0-14-311369-0 (pbk.)
1. Little Bighorn, Battle of the, Mont., 1876   2. Dakota Indians—Wars, 1876.
3. Custer, George Armstrong, 1839–1876.   I. Title.
E83.876.M294   2006
973.8'2—dc22   2006032677

Printed in the United States of America
Set in Cloister   Designed by Francesca Belanger
Maps by Jeffrey L. Ward

For all those who have gone before us.
For all those who taught us how to be Lakota.

Acknowledgments

THANK YOU, first of all, to Carolyn Carlson at Viking Penguin for her patience in waiting for the initial manuscript after my involvement with another project necessitated a delay.

Thank you to Scarecrow Press, Inc., and to the University of Nebraska Press for permission for the use of excerpts: *Shaping Survival: Essays by Four American Indian Tribal Women*, and *Standing Bear and the Ponca Chiefs*, respectively.

As always I am indebted to several elders in the Lakota, Dakota, and Nakota communities primarily in South Dakota who took the time to share their stories and insights with me during my younger days. Though they regarded that sharing as a normal part of the process in a culture that practiced the oral tradition, I regard it as a gift. For many other Lakota people in my generation who listened to stories from our parents' and grandparents' generations, it was a critical insight into the past. We are all grateful for that. Those of us who have been, and are, part of the mechanism of oral tradition must ensure that it continues for one more generation. It is then that generation's responsibility to pass it on. All of us owe that to those who have gone before us and gave us a sense of who and what we are with the stories and lessons they gave to us.

I would like to give a special word of mention regarding the

Discovery Expedition of St. Charles, Missouri. They are the reenactors who, from May 2004 to September 2006, followed the trail of the Lewis and Clark Expedition two hundred years before. Like many native people, I am acutely aware of the difficult and tragic consequences faced and endured by many native tribes and nations over the past two hundred years, as a result of the journey of the Corps of Discovery. Therefore, for me its bicentennial observation is by no means a celebration. However, having gotten to know some of the people who are part of the Discovery Expedition of St. Charles, I can only say that if Lewis and Clark had harbored and demonstrated some of their sensitivity to native peoples, perhaps—just perhaps—history would have been a little different.

A heartfelt appreciation to Viking Penguin for publishing this work, for realizing that there is always another side to the story.

Contents

Preface: Sticks and Stones

THE STORY GOES that an Italian explorer landed on an island in the Caribbean and thought he had found India, and called the dark-skinned people he saw *los Indios*. Whatever the details or the veracity of the story, the consequence is that all the native peoples of North America, Central America, and South America are known to most of the world as Indians. Throw in political correctness and there continues to be confusion over what to call whom, and at what time.

There are, of course, several less complimentary names that were coined and are still around, but the most persistent generic labels (which we all seem to slap on one another) are Indian, American Indian, and Native American. I should note that these labels are used less frequently by those of us shoved into them. We prefer to be identified by our specific tribes or nations, of which there are nearly five hundred ethnically identifiable in the United States.

However, in the interest of avoiding confusion within the pages of this work, I have chosen to use the word *Indian* mostly in those instances when there is a necessary reference to more than a specific tribe or native nation. (I cannot help myself; perhaps it is the English-speaking portion of my brain.) And there are instances when I will use the word *native* for the same reason.

I will avoid using the labels American Indian or Native American, except in those cases where they are part of historical documents or statements.

Native American seems to be the most popular label these days. However, as several people have pointed out to me over the years, anyone born of American parents within the borders of the United States of America or its territories is a *native* American. I quite agree. Furthermore, within the context of historical time frames, much of the content of this work focuses on the Lakota people before we were granted citizenship by the United States Congress in 1924; therefore it seems silly to me to refer to the Lakota (and any other native group) as Native American.

There are no references herein to the people of India, who are, of course, the real Indians. I extend my apologies to them for being dragged into this confusion over labels. But then, neither they nor anyone from North, South, or Central America started this confusion. We are simply forced to live with it, and sometimes answer for it.

Introduction

WHERE ARE YOU FROM?

We all have heard that question more than we probably realize. More often than not we respond with the name of the place where we reside or where we were born or raised. That is, of course, the most obvious and seemingly logical answer.

Yet there is one place where we are all from, no matter our race or ethnicity or social status.

We are all from the past.

Who and what we are is shaped and influenced not only by the blood of our parents, grandparents, and ancestors, but also by their values, traditions, customs, and attitudes—and by the events they witnessed and experienced. How we view the world today, as well as our individual, racial, and societal circumstances, depends on what happened to our ancestors, on what they did or did not do, and on what they suffered or perpetrated. Therefore, in order to understand ourselves, we must endeavor to understand who and what our ancestors were. We must understand our past.

Like many people—and perhaps more than some—I, as a Lakota, struggle to answer one of many questions: Why? Why did our history, especially in the past two hundred years, happen the way it did?

The answers obviously lie in the past and in the people who were part of it and know of it.

There are many photographs of Lakota people from the latter part of the nineteenth century. Whether or not we are directly descended from anyone in those photographs, we should realize that they were more than individuals isolated in a moment. They had substance to them that the photographs only hint at. They had experiences, values, ideas, character, and much more. And some of what and who they were outlived them because someone remembered something they said and did. And that memory can be just as powerful as a photograph, because part of that person was passed on, and is passed on each time a story is told.

Interestingly, one of my favorite stories is about a non-Lakota ancestor. At least by blood he was not Lakota. My paternal grandfather's father was a Frenchman. His name was Joseph. He married a young Oglala Lakota woman, my great-grandmother Elizabeth. They had a home and made a life for themselves on the Pine Ridge Reservation. My great-grandfather worked as an interpreter for the Indian Bureau; he could speak French, English, Lakota, and perhaps a smattering of Cheyenne. As a younger man he had been a horse trader. He was also a teacher and later became an ordained Episcopal deacon.

My great-grandfather was sitting with several old Lakota friends one day shortly after 1900, near the issue station at Pine Ridge Agency. The conversation was about horses, so he told them a story of a good fast horse he had owned as a young man.

One day he happened to find an old, part-log, part-sod house hidden in a small valley in the Medicine Root district of the reservation. Curious, he dismounted from his horse and went inside to have a look. The house was empty and obviously abandoned. As he emerged from it, he saw three riders approaching: three young Lakota men he did not recognize. They saw a white man alone in a remote part of the reservation and loped down the hill toward him.

My great-grandfather quickly mounted his horse, not sure what the men would do if they caught him. He put his horse into a fast gallop and soon outdistanced the three pursuers, who gave up the chase realizing they had no chance of catching him. His horse was too fast for them.

When my great-grandfather finished his story, a man sitting nearby stood up and approached. He had been listening with great interest. "What he says is true," the man told everyone in the group. "I was one of those three riders, and I remember that horse."

Stories do have a way of connecting us. We may not have photographs of all of our ancestors, but we do have stories. Sometimes those stories can reveal things a two-dimensional image cannot. They can reveal a person's character, for example, because they look behind the image into the heart and soul.

I often wonder about the kind of people our ancestors were. What compelled them to cross the Great Muddy River and walk onto the northern plains? What was it about them that enabled them to survive in an environment where others had failed? Was it because they were tough to begin with, or did the plains teach them how to be strong?

As those questions have formed and floated through my mind, I have realized where to find the answers. When I was a child and young person, the answers were all around me in the stories of my parents, my grandparents, and the community of Lakota people in the Swift Bear and Horse Creek communities on the Rosebud Reservation, and around Kyle on the Pine Ridge Reservation, where more answers continue to be revealed.

Several years ago the discovery of human remains on the Rosebud Reservation by highway engineers brought to mind a story of an encounter between Sicangu Lakota and some Pawnee. It likely occurred around 1800 because both the Pawnee and the Sicangu had firearms at the time. The Pawnee, less than a dozen, were raiding for horses into our territory but were discovered and chased by a larger force of Sicangu.

A running battle ensued until the Pawnee were able to gain a high ridge not far from the Smoking Earth (now Little White) River, in what is the north central portion of the Rosebud Reservation, and dig in. The Sicangu surrounded the ridge, and the encounter turned into a siege that went on for days. It was a difficult fight. A Sicangu was seriously wounded (or perhaps even killed) and two of the Pawnee were also killed. After a few days, the raiders were out of water and food. When the Sicangu fighters signaled for a parley, the Pawnee accepted.

Communicating mostly by hand sign, the Sicangu offered to let the Pawnee live if they gave up their guns and horses. The Pawnee agreed, but they asked to be allowed to dig deeper graves for their dead comrades, and that the remains not be molested. Because the Pawnee had fought hard, out of respect for their courage the Sicangu agreed.

When the burials were finished, the Pawnee turned over their guns and horses, and the Sicangu escorted them to the Running

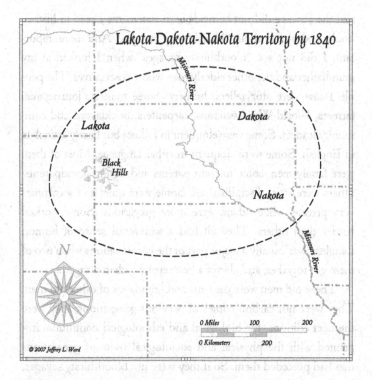

Water (now Niobrara) River, the southern border of their territory, and set them free.

I first heard this story as a boy and was immediately drawn to it because it was about warriors pitted in a death struggle with one another. Later on I realized that it was just as much about compassion as it was about courage. I do not know if the pieces of human remains the engineers found were the Pawnee from that story. But in my heart I believe they are because the veracity of Lakota oral tradition cannot be ignored.

Somehow the outcome of that encounter between the Sicangu

and the Pawnee did not coincide with statements I read in history books and novels about "bloodthirsty savages." And more important, I did not see "bloodthirsty savages" when I looked at my grandfather and the other elderly men who were relatives. The people I saw were storytellers, hunters, horse trainers, journeyman farmers, World War I veterans, carpenters, bricklayers, and community leaders. Some were eloquent in Lakota but barely articulate in English. Some were eloquent in either language. Most of them were family men, some tolerant parents and doting grandparents; others were strict disciplinarians. Some were quiet and sometimes very private, while others were more gregarious. Some worked harder than others. They all had a wonderful sense of humor. Laughter was usually a major part of the conversations when two of them got together, and always when several gathered together.

These old men were the sons and grandsons of other old men. They were not carbon copies of previous generations; they were the next editions, the biological and ethnological continuum imprinted with the physical and sociological traits of generations that had preceded them. So if they were not bloodthirsty savages, I reasoned as a young man, then perhaps there were none in their family trees.

And then there were the mothers and grandmothers.

An unspoken sentiment, which should have been spoken often, certainly sums up the female contribution to Lakota culture: *Wica kin woecun wokokpeke kin ecunpi. Winyan kin ins ecunpicasni kin ecunpe.* Loosely translated, it means, "Men did the dangerous work, and women did the impossible."

My grandmother could wield an ax as well as any man. She toiled in the hot sun as much as my grandfather did. Lakota women of her generation knew how to work hard, and they did.

As a boy, I helped my grandmother haul water. She carried two buckets. My boyhood memories also include digging for *tinpsila* (now called wild turnips) under the hot August sun with my mother and grandmother. Knocking down buffalo berries was no easy task either. Buffalo berry trees had thorny branches, so the fruit could not be picked by hand. Branches had to be struck repeatedly with a long stick to shake the berries down onto a piece of cloth beneath the tree. Then the berries had to be washed, sorted, and dried.

It is not difficult, then, to believe the stories of Lakota women who, just two generations before me, could take down a buffalo-hide lodge in half an hour or less, and then pitch it again just as quickly. But the role of women in prereservation Lakota culture required much more than physical toughness. Not only did they keep the home, they also kept the family. They were the first influence, and the first teachers, of the children in the household and the extended family. Their influence was the foundation for the growth of children and young people into responsible and caring adults. The emotional strength and nurturing support of mothers, grandmothers, and aunts enabled families to function and survive within the parameters of the environment, and to thrive as a community.

In a time and an environment where circumstances could change in a heartbeat, whether because of an enemy attack or a sudden storm, women did their part to ensure the safety and well-being of the family and community. Where men behaved (usually) with decisive action, women were the calming, reassuring influence. I could see that in all my grandmothers, and I can see it in my mother, who is in her eighth decade. To be sure, there was a variety of personalities and character traits as well.

Some old women were known for their sharp tongues, or the twinkle in their eyes, or perhaps a penchant for roll-your-own cigarettes. But all of them were reflections of past generations.

Looking at the culture embodied in my grandparents' generation, I believe it is obvious that Lakota life before reservations was very good. No one had to teach us family values, spiritual strength, love of country, religion, respect for elders, or convince us that there is a God. No one had to teach our Lakota ancestors about the institution of marriage, or the value of wisdom, or that kindness to others is more important than material wealth. These things, and so much more, we had figured out for ourselves.

Migrating onto the northern plains and physically surviving was not easy by any means. Neither was adapting to the reservation after generations of living as free-roaming nomads. Yet it is obvious that the same strength, tenacity, and stubbornness that enabled our Lakota ancestors to adapt and thrive on the plains also enabled their descendants to survive difficult change.

My great-grandparents were part of that continuum of survival. They were born in the 1855–60 era and knew the pain of losing their freedom and the confusion of adapting. My grandparents were born just before 1890 and a few years after, at the beginning of the reservation era, and heard firsthand accounts of that loss and their parents' adaptation to an unwanted lifestyle. As sad as they must have been to hear the stories, they could know only intellectually of the circumstances experienced by their parents. In spite of that, they understood that their parents' experience had brought about the ones that existed for them.

The stories from one generation to the next have linked us together. And each generation has taken its inspiration from the previous one, standing on its strength and stubbornness, and a core of the culture its values helped to preserve.

That, in a nutshell, is where my generation of Lakota comes from.

Even within the context of any situation that is as we want it to be, change does occur. The photographs of Lakota people taken in the late nineteenth and early twentieth century were of people in the midst of change. The world as they knew it had ended. They did not embrace the change, but they did meet it head on. They did so not because there was virtually no other choice, but because who and what they were as people would not allow them to do otherwise.

During that era, several of my ancestors were photographed. One of them was my maternal great-grandfather, Matthew Good Voice Eagle. He was a healer, a medicine man, and my maternal grandmother's father. He was photographed with a pipe in his hands, symbolizing that he would hold on to his Lakota beliefs. And that he did. He died young, at forty-nine, and the family stories say he did not want his body placed in a casket. So he was buried wrapped in blankets and robes. My grandmother said he wanted nothing to prevent his body from returning to the earth in the way that it was meant to.

Another photograph is of one of my paternal grandmothers, Katie Roubideaux Blue Thunder, taken when she was eight years old. She is wearing a buckskin dress, leggings, and beaded moccasins, and she is holding a stuffed doll as she stands in front of a studio backdrop. The look on her face hints at the indomitable spirit with which she lived her life. She was a widow twice and raised children as well as grandchildren, and was a great-grandmother. Her earthly journey ended one month short of her one hundred and first birthday. When Grandma Katie was about ninety years old, her daughter (my aunt Rhoda) wondered who would take care of her when she was old. To which Grandma Katie said, "Do not worry, I will take care of you."

The people in those kinds of photographs are part of who we are as Lakota. And although there are many, many photographs, there are infinitely more stories. They range from humorous to tragic, and while we like to laugh rather than cry, we need to connect with those who have gone before by becoming aware—as much as possible—of the road they walked. And after we have laughed and cried, we will have a better insight into who and what we are. Furthermore, if we expect anyone in the generations to come to listen to our stories, we need to listen to those who have gone before us. In that way we pass on more than just ourselves or our current generations. In that way we can be the linchpin between the past and the future.

So while all of those photographs are important, they are only a surface image. What lies beneath the surface is the substance—the heart, mind, and soul—of those people, our ancestors. That substance is part of what we are, and it is contained in stories. And those stories tell us where we are from and will guide us on the roads that lie ahead.

The Day the World Ended
at Little Bighorn

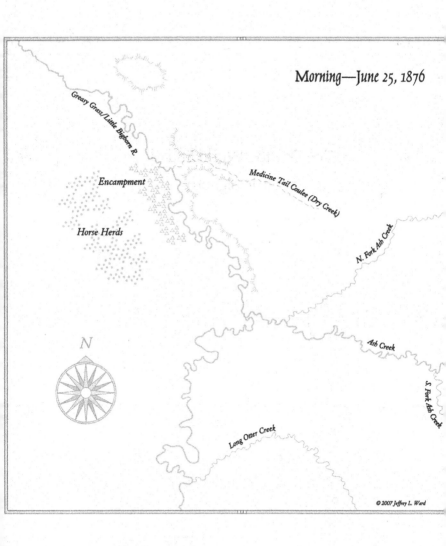

Morning—June 25, 1876

Greasy Grass/Little Bighorn R.

Encampment

Horse Herds

Medicine Tail Coulee (Dry Creek)

N. Fork Ash Creek

Ash Creek

S. Fork Ash Creek

Long Otter Creek

N

© 2007 Jeffrey L. Ward

The Greasy Grass Fight, or the Battle
of the Little Bighorn, June 1876

"Soldiers falling into camp . . ."

IN FORMATION, they charged across a broad and open flood-plain just west of the river called the Little Bighorn. A line of men on horses headed directly for the southern end of the en-campment of nearly a thousand lodges and eight thousand peo-ple. At some point in the headlong gallop, the attacking soldiers opened fire. Blasts of gunfire shattered the relative stillness of the hot afternoon.

Bullets from the first scattered volleys easily reached the camp. Their first kills were not combatants, however. Two women and a girl were the first casualties of the Battle of the Little Bighorn. They happened to be the wives and a daughter of a capable and re-spected battle leader among the Hunkpapa Lakota. Their deaths would motivate him to fight "like a wounded bear," and he would have a decisive role in the second engagement that was yet to come.

On the Lakota calendar, this pivotal day was toward the end of the month called Wipazuke Waste Wi, or the Month When Berries Are Good. On the calendar used by the attackers, it was June 25, 1876.

The soldiers did not achieve total surprise, however, as had been their intent. A lone Lakota, traveling east, crossed a ridge southeast of the river and saw the dust column raised by hundreds of moving horses. He raced back to the camp with a warning, reaching it moments before the advancing cavalry fired their first shots.

Spurred by the warning and the firing, the people in the encampment reacted swiftly. Fighting men grabbed their weapons and caught their horses or any horse that was close, while their women and children and elderly fled north and west away from the gunfire.

The defenders hurried toward the south end, where the Hunkpapa Lakota had pitched their lodges. Some were on foot and many others were mounted, but they all hurried toward the gunfire. Initially, less than a hundred men emerged from the brush and trees to meet the broad front of soldiers moving toward the encampment, but more and more arrived until their numbers at least equaled the attackers', somewhere between 120 and 175. Those with firearms opened fire immediately.

Inexplicably, it seemed to the Lakota fighters, the soldiers stopped and dismounted. The horses of two soldiers, however, became uncontrollable and carried their riders on a mad dash through the outer line of defenders, and then to the outer edges of the encampment. Angry people, including a number of women, surrounded and pulled the hapless riders from their horses, and quickly dispatched them. Thus, the vision received weeks earlier by Hunkpapa Lakota medicine man Sitting Bull during the Sun Dance—the most holy of Lakota ceremonies—was, in part, literally fulfilled. He had seen dying soldiers and their horses falling headfirst from the sky into a Lakota camp. Soldiers falling into camp became a watchword for victory.

The other soldiers in the skirmish line were now essentially

Reno Attacks—Custer Proceeds North

foot soldiers. Meanwhile, more and more mounted fighters emerged from the encampment. All the while, the exchange of gunfire was steady.

Several battle leaders arrived and conferred, among them Gall of the Hunkpapa Lakota and Crazy Horse of the Oglala Lakota. It was Gall whose wives and daughter had been killed. He decided to lead a charge—probably stemming from outrage at his loss—against the western end of the skirmish line, where most of the cavalry's Indian scouts were deployed. The line collapsed quickly and a rout ensued.

In the face of the mounted charge, some of the soldiers ran, and others remounted and fled south and then east toward the river, and took shelter in a thick grove of trees. The Lakota and Cheyenne infiltrated the soldiers' disorganized lines as they retreated, exacting casualties with a point blank shot or the deadly swing of a war club. Once the soldiers gained the shelter of the trees, they were immediately surrounded and intense fighting ensued. Using brush fires and arrows in addition to concentrated gunfire, the Lakota drove the soldiers out of the trees, forcing them to flee east and across the river. In that action, the soldiers suffered more casualties. The Lakota and Cheyenne were in their element as mounted fighters in close combat, and by now their numbers had increased to two or three hundred.

There was no respite for the soldiers as they were relentlessly pursued up the opposite slope. Gaining a grassy ridge a few hundred yards above the river, they were able to establish a defensible position and put up hasty barricades of equipment. A few of the soldiers managed to dig rifle pits. The attackers had now become defenders.

Messengers reached the battle leaders among the Lakota as

Reno Retreats—Custer Arrives
at Medicine Tail Coulee

Greasy Grass/Little Bighorn R.

Encampment

Horse Herds

Medicine Tail Coulee (Dry Creek)

N. Fork Ash Creek

Ash Creek

N

S. Fork Ash Creek

Long Otter Creek

© 2007 Jeffrey L. Ward

Custer   Reno

now more fighting men had joined the fray, and many were surrounding the beleaguered soldiers, preparing to overrun them.
A new threat had come from the north.

Scores of Lakota and Cheyenne fighters left the ridge.
Enough were left to keep the soldiers pinned down behind their
barricades as others raced north, some along the ridges and some
through the encampment.

Thus ended the Valley Fight, as it would come to be known,
the first engagement of the Battle of the Little Bighorn, with
heavy losses for the soldiers and an outcome probably none of
them had expected.

"As long as it takes the sun to move between two lodge poles"

BY THE TIME the encampment's fighting men had chased the soldiers up to the ridge above the river, many of the noncombatants—
women, children, and elderly—had gotten away to the west and
north of camp. Some found hiding places, such as a thicket, and
waited, prepared to flee again at a moment's notice. A few had even
managed to take down lodges and load them on drag poles behind
horses. Up and down the wide, shallow valley, the sound of gunfire
was nearly continuous.

Upstream from the north end of the encampment, a broad
gully opened to the east, following a dry creek. It was known as
Dry Creek and Medicine Tail Coulee. There was a river crossing known to many, including the Crow and Arikara scouts who
rode with the soldiers. As the fighting continued to the south, a
few old men and teenage boys took up positions in shrubs and
sandbar willows on the western side of the river and watched the

crossing. And it was at that crossing where the second engagement of the battle began.

As some of the old men had anticipated, soldiers did come to the crossing. A line of them approached the water and paused, perhaps because the stream was deep because of the mountain snow runoff. Then one in the lead urged his horse into the water, followed by a few others. The old men and boys in the willows opened fire, hitting the lead soldier. Other soldiers immediately went to his aid, some returned fire, and all effected a hasty retreat back to the far bank and beyond. Shortly thereafter, the entire column of soldiers—at least as many as had attacked from the south—turned north and went at a gallop up a long slope.

No sooner had the echo of the muzzle-loading rifles from the small band of ambushers in the willows faded away than mounted Lakota and Cheyenne splashed across the river in pursuit of the soldiers. Many of them had come from routing the first group of attackers. Some had weapons and ammunition captured from the Valley Fight. Led by Gall, they followed the soldiers up the slope.

Frenzied activity still gripped the encampment from one end to the other. Someone had seen soldiers on the ridge above the river to the east, and word spread quickly, prompting more women and children to flee northward. To add to the noise and confusion, many of the Lakota and Cheyenne fighters were galloping north through the camp to meet the newest attack.

Even as Gall led the pursuit of the second group of soldiers, Crazy Horse was in the camp gathering warriors to him. He led them north toward an old crossing farther downstream, joined by Two Moons and a contingent of his Cheyenne fighters. They intended to provide a buffer between the soldiers and the fleeing women and children at the very least, and drive the soldiers farther away, if possible.

As Crazy Horse and Two Moons pushed north, Gall and his warriors separated into three columns, one to the right flank of the running soldiers, one to the left, and another behind. Somewhere past the top of the ridge, which stretched for a mile or so and would become known as Battle Ridge, several soldiers stopped and formed a skirmish line to face the oncoming Lakota and Cheyenne. Their firing was effective and slowed the determined pursuit, but they could not stop it entirely. At Gall's bidding, several warriors dismounted, formed their own skirmish line and traded shot for shot with the soldiers in the skirmish line, while a mounted charge bore down on their left flank. The soldier's line collapsed after only a few minutes.

Farther north along the ridge, another soldier commander attempted the same action. But the result was the same. Incoming fire from the pursuing Lakota and Cheyenne was relentless, and their marksmanship was superior to that of the soldiers. The second skirmish line fell back in disarray, and the column of soldiers on the ridge became disorganized, having to fight the advancing Lakota and Cheyenne on two flanks as well as the rear.

At this time in this particular engagement, the only course left to the soldiers was to flee north along the ridge, and all the while they suffered heavy casualties. Crazy Horse, meanwhile, swept farther east and then turned south, and almost immediately encountered a small group of soldiers, forcing them back toward the main body. Then Crazy Horse proceeded south and flanked the now decimated main body of soldiers from the east, or the soldiers' right flank. He led a charge against a particularly determined group, inflicting more casualties.

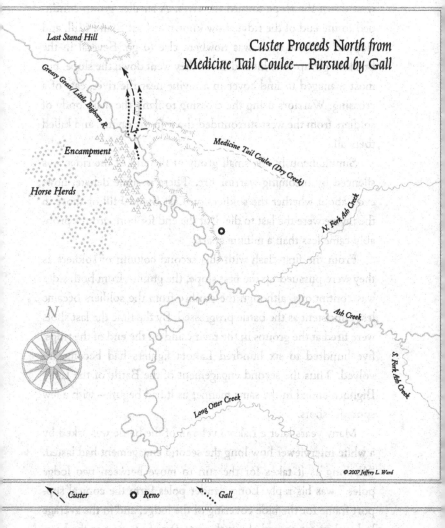

Last Stand Hill

Greasy Grass/Little Bighorn R.

Encampment

Horse Herds

N

Last Stand Hill

**Custer Proceeds North from
Medicine Tail Coulee—Pursued by Gall**

Medicine Tail Coulee (Dry Creek)

N. Fork Ash Creek

Ash Creek

S. Fork Ash Creek

Long Otter Creek

© 2007 Jeffrey L. Ward

↖ Custer   ⊙ Reno   ⋰ Gall

Near the end of the north-south ridge, a number of soldiers—perhaps forty—broke from the main body and headed west down the slope toward the river. A smaller group continued to the end of the ridge, now known as Last Stand Hill, and stopped because there was nowhere else to go. Several in the breakoff group were hit and fell as they went down the slope, but most managed to find cover in a ravine near the river, east of a crossing. Warriors using the crossing to flank the main body of soldiers from the west surrounded those in the ravine, and killed them all.

Simultaneously, the small group at the end of the ridge was silenced by incoming warrior fire. There is some debate, however, about whether the soldiers on Last Stand Hill or those in the ravine were the last to die. But the end for both groups probably came less than a minute apart.

From the first clash with this second column of soldiers as they were pursued up the first slope, the gunfire from both sides was continuous, although the gunfire from the soldiers became less consistent as the battle progressed. By the time the last shots were fired at the groups in the ravine and on the end of the ridge, five hundred to six hundred Lakota fighters had become involved. Thus the second engagement of the Battle of the Little Bighorn ended in the same manner as it had begun—with a few sporadic shots.

Many years later a Lakota veteran of the battle was asked by a white interviewer how long the second engagement had lasted. "As long as it takes for the sun to move between two lodge poles," was his reply. Long slender poles form the conical support frame for the hide covering of the lodge, and in the average lodge they are spaced about three to four feet apart at the base.

As the earth rotates and causes the sun to "move" across the sky, a linear shadow cast by the sun would take about thirty to forty minutes to cross the space between two lodge poles.

"Soldiers on a hill . . ."

SITTING BULL'S VISION had indeed come to pass. Soldiers had attacked a Lakota encampment and were utterly defeated. On the grass- and brush-covered slopes east of the river, the bodies of soldiers and horses dotted the landscape. Every soldier in the second column had been killed. The victorious fighters began claiming the spoils of battle soon after the last angry shot had been fired. People still in the encampment heard shouts of victory punctuated by erratic gunfire and crossed the river to join the celebration.

Among the celebrants were Cheyenne women. One or two of them recognized the braided insignia on the soldiers' uniforms, the same insignia worn by the soldiers who had attacked the camp of the Cheyenne leader Black Kettle at dawn on the Washita River (in 1868) and killed women and children, and captured many as well. Further, some of the Cheyenne women had relatives at Sand Creek (in 1864), where soldiers horribly mutilated women and children after they killed them. Such indelible memories fueled anger and revenge, and many (but not all) of the dead soldiers on the ridges and slopes above the Little Bighorn were mutilated.

As the victors celebrated, treated the wounded, and gathered up their dead (which were less than forty overall), warning shots and the shrill call of eagle-bone whistles came from the south. The soldiers left on the hill to the south, apparently, were attempting to attack again.

Flush with victory and brimming with confidence, many warriors responded. Nearly two miles south of Battle Ridge, they encountered a mounted column along the sharp, broken hills above the river. A determined charge and sharp exchange of gunfire stopped the attack and drove the soldiers back to their position on the ridge. The warriors watching the soldiers on the hill reported that yet a third column of soldiers had come from the southeast. But even with the new arrivals, the soldiers were still outnumbered by the Lakota and Cheyenne fighters. Other attempts to attack were easily beaten back.

It was late afternoon, though the sun was still high. Lakota and Cheyenne warriors dispersed around the soldiers' position, working their way through what little cover there was in the form of sagebrush and the occasional depressions and mounds. The soldiers seemed to have plenty of ammunition. In any case, except for a few half-hearted attempts to drive the warriors back, they kept to their position.

The warrior leaders conferred, and scouts were sent out to learn if other soldiers were in the vicinity of the Little Bighorn valley. As the afternoon wore on, the confrontation became flurries of shot-for-shot exchanges, followed by intervals of eerie silence. Only now and then did the wails of wounded soldiers drift from the ridge.

By now the long ridge to the north was deserted, except for turkey buzzards around the dead soldiers. People from the encampment had departed, carrying their wounded and the spoils of victory. In the camp there was excitement as the situation on the ridge across the river settled into a standoff. A few people could not help but celebrate outright, but many did not because many men had been wounded, and some had been killed. But an overall feeling of strength was unmistakable because they had prevailed over their enemy.

As sundown neared, warriors on the outer perimeters of the siege left and returned to the camp for a brief rest, sometimes for water or a quick bite of food, or to reassure their worried families. Throughout the night there would be a somewhat steady flow of men from the siege on the ridge to the camp and back. The old men leaders gathered in the council lodge to talk about what had happened, and what they should do because of it. Many of the battle leaders went to listen, or sent someone to listen for them.

As night fell, scouts began to return. One by one they reported that no other soldier columns had been seen. On the ridge above the river, the heat of the day finally began to dissipate, and cries of the wounded soldiers and telltale noises of movement could be heard. Sometime during the night, a few soldiers sneaked down through the gullies to the river, carrying canteens and other containers for water. Sporadic exchanges of gunfire occurred, but all of the water haulers were able to return to the barricade. Thereafter, the night passed without any further intense or prolonged fighting.

After sunrise, the Lakota and Cheyenne fighters, with a good view of the soldiers' position, could see that they had built a ring of breastworks, made mainly of boxes, saddles, packs, and dead horses. Gunfire disrupted the morning stillness, and the battle was joined once again, and continued into midmorning. A group of young warriors had been gathering to the east of the barricade. A few of them charged close enough to throw stones. To their surprise, a large group of soldiers jumped over the barricade after them, firing their rifles and pistols and inflicting casualties.

The warriors fell back, hoping to draw the soldiers farther out into the open, but the soldiers seemed to realize their predicament and retreated to their position.

Small groups of warriors charged the barricade here and there throughout the morning until about the middle of the day, and each time they were met with determined resistance. But the Lakota and Cheyenne were just as determined to wipe out the soldiers. Sometime in the early afternoon, the warrior leaders passed the word that scouts returning from the north had reported yet another soldier column, a large one, coming south. The plan was to strike the camp and take the women and children to safety into the Shining Mountains to the south. News of more soldiers coming underscored the sentiment that prevailed in the council lodge among the older leaders. Many felt it would be best to withdraw and leave the valley, and let the soldiers on the hill live to tell the story of their defeat at the hands of the Lakota and Cheyenne.

Camp criers (heralds) carried the decision throughout the camp, and a flurry of activity ensued once again. By late afternoon the entire encampment of a thousand households and thousands of horses were ready to move.

Perhaps a hundred or so fighters were left to harass the soldiers and deter any possible pursuit. It seemed, however, that the soldiers were in no condition to do anything but defend themselves behind their breastworks.

Thus ended the Greasy Grass Fight, also known as the Battle of the Little Bighorn.

So the people departed the valley in a long, seemingly endless column, across the very ground where the soldiers had first attacked the day before. The Lakota had come together in the Month When the Horses Shed (May), pitching their first camps near the Chalk Buttes to the east. Sitting Bull had issued a call to gather so that they could talk and discuss what to do to stop the invasion of the whites. They had moved their camps several times until they had come to Ash Creek, not far from the Little Bighorn. A Sun Dance was conducted there to strengthen the people. Later, when their horse herds grazed down the already sparse grass in the Ash Creek drainage, they moved northeast to the Little Bighorn valley. Shortly thereafter, on a hot afternoon, the soldiers had come.

The Lakota claimed the victory and would sing songs of it for generations to come. But as they went away from the Little Bighorn, uneasiness settled in the minds of many of the old ones. In their lifetimes, the whites had gone from annoying and persistent interlopers, like fleas that could not be dislodged, to land-hungry enemies bent on killing the Lakota. That knowledge was the basis for a nagging question that some asked one another, or simply wrestled with alone.

What would this victory bring?

TWO

To and From

SADLY, HOWEVER, not many people today know the true story of the Greasy Grass Fight, more popularly known as the Battle of the Little Bighorn, any more than they know that the story of Lakota and Euro-American interaction began as early as the 1720s.

To Euro-Americans of the day, the Battle of the Little Bighorn was a horrific loss for the U.S. Army. News of the soldiers' defeat came just as the United States was celebrating its centennial. The outrage it sparked was swift and intense.

MASSACRE! screamed the headlines of the *Bismarck Tribune* on July 6, 1876, giving the impression that the soldiers of the Seventh Cavalry were hapless victims. As the story of the battle swept across the nation, the public perception was that a group of savages had inexplicably managed to wipe out the U.S. Army's most elite group of soldiers. That perception remained uncontested for over a hundred years, finding its way into history books, novels, documentaries, and even feature films. Debate still exists today about the outcome of the Battle of the Little Bighorn. The event has been discussed and analyzed from numerous perspectives, and it probably will continue to be. The sad truth is that most people across America and across the world have had access only to the white military version of events, and the assumption is that that is the *only* version.

In fact, the victors of the Little Bighorn have had scant opportunity to tell their story, and many of their individual versions of the battle have been clouded and reshaped by western interpretations, well-meaning or not. "How brave were the soldiers?" asked one magazine writer of a Lakota combatant, sometime in the 1920s. Posed in this manner, the question is leading. The proper question should have been, "Were the soldiers brave?"

This kind of small distinction has tweaked history over time and has prevented the complete account of one of the most important events in western American history from being fairly and objectively reported. Lakota and Cheyenne children, some who were direct descendants of the victors at Little Bighorn, were unabashedly told that the Seventh Cavalry was struck down while trying to "make the West safe for civilization." The story was accentuated, of course, by accounts of Lieutenant Colonel George A. Custer and his gallant soldiers going down in a final blaze of glory—the so-called Last Stand.

Initial disbelief about the Lakota and Cheyenne victory stemmed from a pervasive Euro-American notion that natives were an inferior people. This made it all the more shocking that any American military unit—especially one led by such a heroic figure—could have been defeated.

Most historians would probably assert that we have made significant progress in terms of reporting history objectively. But long-held beliefs do not fade easily. Interpretive rangers (employed by the National Park Service) at the Little Bighorn Battlefield National Monument give battle talks to visitors, describing "Custer's Last Stand." Many of those descriptions extol the soldiers of the

Seventh Cavalry as "heroes in the truest sense of the word." Everyone is entitled to an opinion, of course, even in the interpretation of history, but there is also a duty to the whole truth of history. While the soldiers of the Seventh are heroes to mainstream Americans, they are remembered as despicable enemies to the Lakota and Northern Cheyenne, a fact less often mentioned in the battle talks. Furthermore, in the interest of objectivity, any interpretive presentation should also point out that the Lakota and Northern Cheyenne fighting men were "heroes in the truest sense of the word" to their people.

In the summer of 2005, a battlefield tour guide, speaking to her busload of passengers at the Reno-Benteen barricade site, said, "It was quite by accident that the Lakota gathered here in the summer of 1876." Quite possibly, that busload of tourists left the battlefield with skewed information regarding not only the battle, but the factors that brought it about. The gathering at the Little Bighorn was no accident, and to gain a comprehensive understanding of the battle, it is important to consider both sides of the reality that led to that pivotal event.

Euro-Americans considered natives to be uncivilized savages standing in the path of Christian progress. The Lakota and Northern Cheyenne—who in 1876 were the last holdouts in the northern plains against white incursion—regarded whites as destroyers of their way of life. Therefore, the battle was far from an isolated event. It was the end of the road, the consequence of events, attitudes, emotions, and misunderstandings over the course of several generations. It was the last major battle in a conflict that began when a group of French explorers led by Pierre Gaultier de Varennes, sieur de La Vérendrye, encroached into Lakota territory in the 1720s. They traveled up the Missouri

River and left a lead tablet on a hill overlooking the confluence of the Bad and Missouri Rivers (where present-day Fort Pierre, South Dakota, now sits). They were the first drops in the trickle that led to a flood.

By all accounts, the La Vérendrye group was a belligerent lot, a revealing characteristic because attitude—much more than guns and bullets—was a devastating factor in the conflict. It continues to be. After attitude, the second most effective factor was numbers.

The definitive population of native tribes and nations before the arrival of Europeans is difficult to ascertain. Estimates range from three to ten million people. The Lakota, Dakota, and Nakota alliance reached up to twenty-five thousand people in the mid-1800s, with the Lakota comprising the vast majority (close to twenty thousand). In contrast, at the height of the conflicts during those times, the Lakota faced a Euro-American nation with a population of nearly twenty-five *million*.

Until that fateful summer of 1876, the threat of change had been hanging like a storm cloud over the eastern horizon of Lakota territory for several generations before it finally broke. When it did, the upheaval it brought was like nothing experienced before, primarily because a nation that thought of itself as the epitome of mankind had suffered ignominious defeat at the Little Bighorn.

All in all, the Euro-American consensus was that this outcome was a fluke: the Lakota and Northern Cheyenne were lucky, and the white soldiers were brave and honorable. Hardly mentioned, if ever, were the honor and skill of the native fighters. And they were more formidable. In fact, eight days before the Little Bighorn, the Lakota and Northern Cheyenne fighting

men, led by Crazy Horse, were engaged in a battle along Rosebud Creek against a very large force commanded by Brigadier
General George Crook. The battle ended in a draw in the late afternoon, but it speaks to the skill and fighting abilities of the
Lakota and their Northern Cheyenne allies.

The Battle of the Little Bighorn was not a fluky victory, and
neither was the outcome of the Battle of the Rosebud. The
Lakota and Northern Cheyenne fought hard in both battles and
neutralized two thirds of the forces sent to capture or kill them
that summer. Of course, they were not aware that the United
States Army had a grand plan to catch them in a three-way pincer operation. What they did know was that whites had been in-
vading their territory and affecting their lives for over a century.

There were many consequences of the Euro-American invasion, but the most devastating impact was the loss of the primary
resource on the northern plains: the bison herds. Once seemingly numberless, the bison herds had been reduced to only a
few thousand by the early 1870s. Dire consequences of that reality were felt by all the Lakota, whose physical and spiritual survival depended on this endlessly useful animal. For generations,
bison had been the source of food, clothing, utensils, toys, and
weapons; every part of its body was utilized, from hooves to tail.
At least twenty bison hides were used to construct one conical
dwelling, the *tipestola*, or "pointed dwelling," more commonly
known as the tipi. And its strength and independence were at the
core of the spiritual symbiosis the Lakota shared with it. So long
as the Lakota had bison to eat, they were strong and indepen-
dent. Its decline was both a practical and spiritual blow.

Disease was another negative factor. In 1837, a steamboat traveled northward on the Missouri River with passengers, materials,

and supplies, stopping at various points. One was the Whetstone Landing, near the present town of Pickstown, South Dakota. Something off-loaded from that boat was infected with smallpox. As a result, a devastating epidemic swept through the Lakota, and the Mandan people farther to the north were nearly wiped out that same summer.

The establishment of outposts along the Missouri River, while helpful to travel, trade, and commerce for Euro-Americans, slowly eroded what was left of Lakota territory. Fort Yankton (at present-day Yankton, South Dakota) and Fort Pierre (near present-day Fort Pierre and Pierre, South Dakota) were among the first settlements. Fort John was established in what is now southeast Wyoming, near the North Platte River; first a trading post, it was later purchased by the United States and renamed Fort Laramie, and it became an army post and a significant factor in Lakota life.

The establishment of outposts lured more fur traders and trappers into Lakota territory. Their interaction with the Lakota was basically friendly. They wanted two things: economic gain and information. Land-seeking settlers followed, of course, and then came the soldiers sent to protect them against "threats" from the Lakota. Also in the first groups of Euro-Americans were missionaries whose sole intent was to convert the Lakota to Christianity.

The 1840s brought the Oregon Trail. Though it began in what is now the state of Missouri and ended in Oregon, it crossed through the southern reaches of Lakota territory in what is now northern Nebraska and southern Wyoming. One of the first major conflicts it brought about was the Grattan incident near Fort Laramie, in 1854.

Lieutenant John Grattan, new to Lakota territory, intended

to settle a dispute concerning the loss of a Mormon immigrant's cow in a Sicangu Lakota camp. The Sicangu were encamped near Fort Laramie along with a few other Lakota bands, waiting for the delivery of annuities from the United States, pledged as a result of the 1851 Fort Laramie Treaty. Many of the Sicangu were anxiously awaiting the food rations among the annuities, which were seriously late on this occasion. So when a lone cow, seemingly abandoned, wandered into the Lakota camp and caused havoc, it was subsequently killed and butchered. Only later did the Lakota realize that the cow had a rightful owner.

The owner of the animal demanded reparation. Payment offered by the Sicangu was refused either because it was insufficient or the Mormon owner wanted the animal returned. The latter was, of course, an impossible alternative. The situation escalated when orders were issued for the arrest of the cow killer. To the last possible moment, the Sicangu offered payment of horses and mules. Determined that someone should pay, one way or another, Lieutenant Grattan talked the fort's commander into allowing him to take a detachment of soldiers to the Sicangu camp and settle the matter.

The killer of the cow refused to surrender to the soldiers. His friends and relatives supported this decision. After a confusing verbal exchange, due to the questionable skill and veracity of a half-Lakota (and perhaps drunk) interpreter employed by the army, the situation quickly deteriorated. Grattan opened fire with two mountain howitzers and muzzle-loading rifles from his thirty-man detachment. The Sicangu and Oglala Lakota fighting men in the camp immediately responded, wiping out Grattan and his soldiers in only a few minutes. The incident led to a retaliatory attack by General William Harney a year later. He decimated the camp of the Sicangu Lakota leader Little Thunder on Blue Water Creek (in what is now northwest Nebraska).

Trouble did not end with Harney's campaign, however. In the 1860s, the Bozeman Trail was laid out through the middle of Lakota lands—what is now north central Wyoming—in direct violation of solemn agreements proposed by the Euro-Americans. That trail was a more direct route to gold fields in Montana. Gold was also the reason the Black Hills were invaded in the 1870s.

These and other events put the Lakota in the mood to resist. Lakota outrage was a primary factor that led to the Battle of the Little Bighorn. The Lakota, especially influential leaders such as Sitting Bull, were angered at the extent of Euro-American presence and disruption to their lands and lives. Sitting Bull saw his nation, one that had been so strong for so many generations, weakened by the invasion that diminished territory and resources. It was the culmination of a long and difficult succession of incidents and events that forced the Lakota to realize they needed to do more to defend themselves. This was the road *to* Little Bighorn.

In turn, the outcome of the Battle of the Little Bighorn sparked outrage from the nation that lost it. That nation shaped its outrage into retaliation and caused the victors to walk an exceedingly difficult road *from* the Little Bighorn.

THREE

The Greatest Gathering Ever

NEVER BEFORE, the stories say, and certainly not since, has there been an encampment the size of the Little Bighorn gathering in the summer of 1876. It stretched for two miles along the river, and almost two hundred yards at its widest point. Unless one has stood on the eastern side of the river on a ridge and looked down at the floodplain on the western side, it is difficult to visualize the sheer size.

Too often we look at the trees and grass as we try to imagine the great encampment and marvel at how large it must have been, but we forget the humanity of it. However, for those of us who are Lakota and Sahiyela (Northern Cheyenne), the size of the encampment is not as important as the people who were in it. Those people are our ancestors, our great-grandparents, great-great-grandparents, and great-great-great-grandparents. One can imagine a pair of eyes looking down from the ridges on the east side of the Little Bighorn River to see children, grandmothers and grandfathers, and men and women doing the every day things that were part of their daily lives. Who and what they were and what they did has survived and is part of us modern Lakota and Northern Cheyenne today.

Just before the battle, the encampment along the Little Bighorn had relocated from the site along Ash Creek, some eight miles to the southeast, where it had been for a month or more. Growing numbers of people and horses necessitated the move. The horses had grazed down the grass considerably, so fresh forage was needed for them. When the soldiers attacked, the Little Bighorn encampment had been in place for only a few days.

We have been led to believe that the camp's population was between eight and ten thousand. Demographics of this population cannot be broken down with any dependable specificity. Anecdotal evidence strongly suggests about one thousand lodges in total. Based on that, there would have been eight to ten people in each lodge, but likely less because many single males had separate quarters. But it is probable that females outnumbered males slightly because of losses of males in combat. Any disparity would have been offset by the arrival and presence of single males (mentioned before) and those in camp without their families. Many households consisted of three generations, meaning at least one grandparent. Of the seven Lakota, two Nakota, and four Dakota bands, all were represented, although not equally. A few hundred Sahiyela were also represented. Most numerous were Oglala Lakota, followed by the Hunkpapa and the Sicangu. A number of Northern Arapaho were also present, but most were women married to Lakota or Sahiyela. (A few Northern Arapaho men, it is believed, arrived hours before or just as the soldiers attacked and did eventually participate in the fighting, but not before being held prisoner until their identities were verified.)

The arrangement of the Little Bighorn encampment began with the Hunkpapa at the southern end, then the Itazipacola, Mniconju, Sihasapa, Isanti Dakota, Ihanktunwan Nakota, the

Sicangu and Oohenunpa together, and Oglala and Sahiyela at the northern end. (See map facing page 1.) All around the edges, especially close to the river, were small temporary campsites of unmarried men or men who had come without their families. Near the center were pitched several warrior society lodges and at least one large meeting or council lodge.

The camp was situated among groves of trees, mostly large old-growth cottonwoods, many of which were taller than the tops of the lodge poles. Even from the ridges across the river (as the soldiers realized), it was difficult to see into the encampment.

To the west on the floodplain was the horse herd. We will never know its exact number, but estimates range from twelve to fifteen thousand head. That is a likely figure given that some households owned as many as twenty, and some as few as five. Most of the animals were descendants of the Spanish Barb mustangs, but some had been captured from Euro-Americans. The Lakota-raised horses knew to stay close to encampments because they had been imprinted by human contact within days of birth. From time to time, some people kept young colts inside their lodges. Familiarizing colts as early as possible to human contact with consistent interaction was necessary, because it simply was not feasible for nomadic people to construct corrals at every new encampment. Brood mares were the main part of the herd, not only because they were the source of new colts annually, but also because they learned to stay close to their owners.

To ensure the safety of the herd, horse guards were posted day and night, and especially after the sun went down. During the day, mostly older boys stood guard. At night, older boys and young warriors kept watch around and in the herd.

Adult males between the ages of twenty-five to about forty

usually had at least two warhorses and two buffalo-hunting horses. Very, very rare was the horse that could do it all, because different tasks required different skills and temperament. Sturdier and calmer horses were used as basic transportation for all members of the family, especially for women and the elderly. Each family needed two—and sometimes more—for hauling the dwelling and its accoutrements: lodge poles, covering, lining (dew cloth), chairs, storage containers, and so on. Every male in the family, young or old, had a horse to ride, other than the specialty mounts for hunting and warfare.

The horses in any encampment in any season of the year almost always outnumbered the people. So when eight thousand to ten thousand people came together, it is entirely possible that their horses looked like "maggots in the grass" to scouts looking through a field glass from several miles away.

The material necessities of each family or household almost always included one lodge, several containers for food and clothing and personal items, chairs (also called backrests), sleeping robes, toys for children, tools and utensils used by the women, weapons for hunting and warfare, and ropes and saddles.

The effort and man-hours it took to set up a basic life here is astounding. One lodge cover weighed a few hundred pounds and was made of about twenty to twenty-five buffalo hides sewn together (although several families had canvas lodges). It required an inner lining or dew cloth roughly half the size of the outer covering, sixteen to twenty lodge poles at least twenty feet long, two smoke-flap support poles twenty-five feet or more in length, one smoke-flap peg pole about six feet long, and sixteen to twenty tent pegs about eighteen inches long. Pegs were attached to loops at the bottom edge of the cover and pounded into the ground to keep the lodge secure, even in the strongest winds.

The most common type of containers were made of rawhide, that is, the hides of deer and elk that had been soaked and scraped of hair. They were of various sizes, rectangular in shape, and painted with intricate geometric designs, and folded like envelopes. Those used to store food contained dried meat, dried fruits, and dried vegetables. Several were used to store clothing. Ceremonial objects, such as feather headdresses, were kept in cylindrical containers, as were personal items, such as hairbrushes for women and girls. Most families needed six to a dozen containers, sometimes more, including water flasks of some type.

Willow chairs were a common and necessary item of furniture in every household. Constructed of thin willow rods tied in lattice fashion, they were about five to six feet long and supported by a tripod of sturdy poles. At least four or five in each dwelling were not unusual. They are now known as backrests because the person using one sat on the bottom third, and leaned back against the two thirds affixed to the tripod. The Lakota word *oakanke*, or "something to sit on," describes the use of this piece of furniture. But it later referred to the four-legged chair when the people began using it on a regular basis.

Numerous robes from deer, elk, and buffalo were also used, some for floor covering but most for bed covering. Though by 1876, many families owned and used wool blankets provided in the treaty annuity payments by the United States government. There could be as many as ten to two dozen robes and blankets.

Households with children had toys: dolls made from soft hides and stuffed with grass for girls, miniature bows and arrows for boys, and several types of hand toys to teach hand-eye coordination and alleviate the tedium of long winter nights. And there were various animals made from the vertebrae bones of deer, elk, and bison. Toys had their containers, of course.

Just as important as toys were the various tools used by men and women. Men's tools were the kind necessary for weapons construction and repair, such as arrow straighteners. Women had a wider variety of tools, including sewing awls, hide scrapers, and by 1876, steel needles and knives with metal blades. Cooking utensils included large and small cast-iron pots, metal cups and dishes, butcher knives, and, still, a few wooden spoons. Many households, especially with elderly present, preferred buffalo-horn spoons and cups.

Because every adult male was a hunter and most males were fighting men, weapons for hunting and warfare were part of every household. Every man had at least one bow for hunting and one for combat, and many had several of each. Hunting arrows and war arrows were different in design, so there were at least two quivers of arrows, often more. Likewise, buffalo-hunting lances were different from war lances, though by this time in history men who had rifles rarely used lances of any kind, except for ceremonies. Buffalo-hide shields, war clubs of various materials and designs, and riding quirts were also necessary items. There were, of course, various types of firearms. Fortunate was the man who had a rifle of some kind and a pistol as well.

Women used saddles more often than men, so it was not unusual for each household to have a saddle for every adult female. Saddles were made of buffalo bones and rawhide, though various types captured from the military or white civilians were not uncommon. Other horse accoutrements were braided-hair ropes, reins, rawhide hobbles, braided soft-leather halters, and a scattering of iron-bit bridles.

Obviously, some households had more possessions than others, but by and large each had several hundred pounds and sometimes as much as a ton of items. It was largely the responsibility of the women to organize, and to pack and unpack. The biggest chore was to dismantle the lodge. That meant taking off the outer covering and inner liner, folding them into transportable bundles, and taking down the lodge poles. This was not easy work by any means, but teams of women working together were able to take down, or strike, a lodge in less than half an hour, and they were able to put it up at a new location in about the same time.

To put the physical and material aspects of the Little Bighorn encampment in a broader perspective, consider the numbers:

- A minimum 1,000 lodge coverings and nearly as many inner liners
- 16,000 to 20,000 lodge poles
- 16,000 to 20,000 ground pegs
- 5,000 to 6,000 buffalo, elk, and deer hides
- 5,000 to 7,000 containers of various types
- 3,000 to 5,000 chairs (backrests)
- 1,000 (at least) cast-iron kettles
- 2,000 to 3,000 water flasks
- 25,000 pounds, or 12.5 tons, of dried meat (25 pounds per household)
- 10,000 to 15,000 pounds, or 5.0 to 7.5 tons, of dried fruits and vegetables

- thousands of toys
- hundreds of saddles
- thousands of ropes and other horse accoutrements
- thousands of weapons

This list does not include approximately 2,000 pounds, or one ton, of fresh meat per day that was needed and consumed, or at least 4,000 gallons of fresh water consumed each day. As far as the horses were concerned, if each adult consumed twenty pounds of forage per day, the entire herd was capable of consuming a staggering 100 to 150 *tons* of hay *per day.*

Obviously, an encampment of eight to ten thousand people and ten to fifteen thousand horses was an enormous drain on the surrounding ecosystem. The older leaders, like Sitting Bull, were well aware of this fact and knew that such a large group of people could not stay together indefinitely. This would prove to be a problem.

For many years, and with growing alarm, Sitting Bull and other leaders among the Lakota watched the consistent and unwelcome incursion of white people into Lakota territory. Though the Lakota did resist, they could not do enough to stem the tide.

Then in late 1875, the Grant administration, at the urging of generals William Sherman and Philip Sheridan, issued an ultimatum that all Indians should report to reservations by January 31, 1876, or risk being considered "hostile." The government of the United States was giving itself a reason—and legal authority in its own eyes—to force Indians onto reservations. It knew that leaders like Sitting Bull and Crazy Horse would ignore the ultimatum, even if they could understand it. And they were, by far, the most influential Lakota leaders.

Early in 1876, Sitting Bull sent out his own message. He wanted a gathering of the people and their leaders. He wanted to talk with them about the fact that more and more whites were moving into Lakota lands. And gather they did. The first groups came together around late April and early May near the Chalk Buttes in what is now southeastern Montana. There were a few hundred at first, but the numbers gradually grew. By the time they arrived near Ash Creek, about 150 miles west of the Chalk Buttes, there were a few thousand. The encampment grew steadily thereafter. By the time Sitting Bull conducted his Sun Dance, there were over six thousand people present. By the time Crazy Horse left the Ash Creek camp on June 17 to attack General Crook on the Rosebud, the number was closer to eight thousand, if not more.

The Sun Dance was held earlier in the season than usual: late June to early August. Sitting Bull's concerns warranted the slight break in tradition. No one took any exception worth noting, especially after Sitting Bull reported a vision that foretold victory. During the ceremony, he had gone into a trance and seen soldiers and their horses falling from the sky, headfirst into a Lakota encampment, with their ears cut off. Soldiers falling into camp became the watchword for victory because Sitting Bull was a powerful medicine man. He told the people that "they have no ears," meaning the white soldiers would not listen. Therefore, it would be necessary to teach them a lesson.

A warning came with the vision, however. A victory over the soldiers was assured, Sitting Bull was certain. But the victors were not to claim any spoils from the victory. (In the aftermath of the Battle of the Little Bighorn, many warriors and noncombatants did not heed the warning, and they stripped the soldiers of clothing and weapons.)

Since Sitting Bull had called for the gathering, he made the most of the opportunity to speak with his contemporaries—men of influence as well as those from prominent families. He made sure that the topic of the day always related to the problem of white incursion. Since many of the people had left the agencies (reservations) to attend the gathering, Sitting Bull worked hard to convince them that a concerted effort to fight off the white people was their best hope.

Meanwhile, life at the encampment went on. Wise old leaders debated the ever-growing specter of white encroachment, but children played, young men courted their hearts' desire, babies were born, and the elderly died. Warriors were inducted into societies, and men traded horses. Boys and young men raced their horses. Some fell off and scraped elbows and bruised egos. Old men sat in gray and white-haired enclaves and traded stories, and old women visited with relatives. Marriages were arranged as hearts were filled to bursting, or broken. Medicine men healed the sick and prayed for departed souls. Scouts rode off to the four directions to watch for enemies. Hunters searched the prairies and stalked in the mountains to bring home fresh meat.

Some of the people remembered an autumn and winter eleven years earlier when they had come together with many of their Sahiyela and Arapaho friends and relatives. That had been along the Shell (North Platte) River far to the south, in the shadow of Elk Mountain. They had fought the soldiers at Platte Bridge Station. That encampment, many agreed, was large but not nearly as large as the gathering at Ash Creek and the Little Bighorn.

So at Ash Creek and again at the Little Bighorn, the grand-mothers and grandfathers beseeched their children and grandchil-dren to remember. Given the changes occurring, many feared that such a gathering might never happen again.

Though the Lakota and Northern Cheyenne lived the fulfill-ment of Sitting Bull's vision and fought hard for their victory, some of them sensed that difficult changes would be part of their future. As the Reno-Benteen soldiers watched from the hill, a long, long line of Lakota and Northern Cheyenne walked and rode away toward the Shining (Big Horn) Mountains to the south. And even as they went, the people sang songs and told stories not only of their triumph, but also of the great gathering as well.

That *was* the greatest gathering ever in the era before reserva-tion borders and square walls. The difficult changes did come; and some consequences still linger, and some have darkened Lakota dreams. But the songs are still sung, and the stories are still told.

FOUR

In the Beginning

The Titunwan

WHILE THE ENCAMPMENT along the Little Bighorn was the largest ever in terms of numbers—and was the last—it certainly was not the first. The Lakota had come together in large encampments before, and the primary reasons were to affirm their existence, their beliefs, their sense of self, and their place in the world—and to renew it all with ceremonies and by reconnecting with friends and relatives. So gathering together was a long-standing tradition.

But how had that tradition—and all the others—come to be? How had the people themselves come to be?

There is always a beginning.

No one knows exactly when our Lakota ancestors crossed the Missouri River, or the Great Muddy, as they called it, but it was perhaps as late as 1680. It was the time before horses, so they crossed on foot, probably in the winter when the river was frozen solid. Whenever they crossed, the vast, endless prairies and bison—too numerous to count on those western hinterlands—were much to their liking. The horse had yet to arrive, but it soon would.

The first groups showed the way for those who followed. Their encampments were small, probably no more than ten to twenty families, and each was no more than half a day's travel away from at least two or three others, often less. As the seasons and the years passed, they moved over the land and came to know it well.

In the era before horses, the tipi was much smaller. Its appearance was much the same as its posthorse version: a conical-shaped hide covering supported by straight poles. Its floor space was no more than ten to twelve feet across, and it was taller than a man, about eight feet high at its center. Because of the small space, families were small in number, no more than four or five.

Much of the prereservation Lakota society that had been established was in place long before they moved onto the prairies. They were able to survive and flourish because they had well-defined roles for both males and females. Tasks were divided logically to meet the needs for surviving as a nomadic hunting society. At the time, women were better suited for some tasks that men were not, and vice versa.

Women were the caretakers of home and family and the first teachers and nurturers of children. Chores such as cooking, gathering firewood, child care, sewing, hide tanning, and so on, were their responsibility. Most important, as nurturers of the family unit, they had a profound impact on all of the children in the household and the extended family, and even from birth because midwives attended the birth of every child whenever possible. Overall, women shaped the basic values and attitudes of all children, male and female. There was no greater responsibility than that. As a matter of fact, there was an ancient premise that young men learned the skills to be hunters and warriors from their fathers and grandfathers, but they learned compassion and courage from their mothers and grandmothers.

Men, on the other hand, were better suited for the roles of providers and protectors. Those responsibilities, especially as the hunter, took men away from home. Beneath the broad societal roles of hunter and warrior, men necessarily fulfilled other roles. Like women, they were teachers, teaching hunting, fighting, and survival skills to boys and young men. They were also husbands, fathers, and grandfathers, and some attained positions of military and civilian leadership. Some became medicine men.

These gender roles evolved over time, and this social structure helped the Lakota to adapt to life on the northern plains and to succeed there where others had failed.

The Lakota were already an old nation with an established lifestyle when they migrated to the northern plains. They were nomadic hunters. On the plains they discovered there was no choice but to move with the rhythm of the seasons, and the great animal that would become a critical physical resource—the buffalo (bison).

Buffalo were not unknown to the Lakota. Like wolves and grizzly bears, buffalo were widespread across the continent, a seemingly inexhaustible source of food and shelter. But there was also a spiritual connection. The seven sacred ceremonies at the core of Lakota spiritual beliefs and religious practices were brought to them by the White Buffalo Calf Maiden hundreds and perhaps thousands of years before. Those ceremonies are as follows:

- *Hanbleceyapi*, or "crying for a vision," the vision quest
- *Inikagapi*, or "making new life," commonly called the sweat lodge ceremony

- *Nagi gluhapi na gluskapi,* or "keeping and releasing the spirit"
- *Isna alowanpi,* or "over her alone, they sing," a puberty rite for young women
- *Hunka,* or "the making of peace," sometimes called "making a relative"
- *Tapa wankayeyapi,* or "tossing the ball," the second ceremony for women
- *Wiwanyang wacipi,* or "watching the sun and dancing," the Sun Dance

Further, a creation or re-creation story describes how the buffalo once lived beneath the earth. When *she* looked out upon the Earth, the Lakota were suffering immensely from starvation. So she came up out of the ground and became many. The Lakota hunted and ate of her flesh.

Interestingly, the Lakota refer to themselves as Pte Taoyate, or the Buffalo Nation, or "her nation," since the designation for the female is used. *Tatanka* is the word for the male buffalo, and *pte* means the female.

The buffalo as a vital resource was widely known, of course, to other native people, including the Kiowa and Cheyenne, who are believed to have already been living on the plains west of the Missouri. The Kiowa were a small group who relented to the pressure of more aggressive people and eventually moved south, to end up in what is now Kansas. As for the Cheyenne, they initially resisted, but in time became friends and allies of the Lakota.

Remaining among the rivers and rolling lands east of the Missouri were the other people of the nation, the Dakota and

Nakota. They were hunters like their Lakota relatives, but they were also planters and gatherers and liked the fertile bottomlands. They labeled their far-roaming Lakota relatives the Titunwan, or People of the Prairies. Though the great river divided them geographically, the three groups would remain staunch allies. Of course, when the harsh northern plains winters froze the Missouri, many people crossed it to visit relatives on both sides.

The other alliance the entire nation had was with the dog, or *sunka*. It was both companion and beast of burden. In the beginning of this relationship, somewhere in the mists of time, the dog emerged as a domesticated version of the coyote and the wolf. The coyote showed more of a knack for adjusting to a new lifestyle, and his disposition was preferable in crossbreeding. But it was the wolf's size and strength that the Lakota needed to carry their belongings. Though the Lakota were able to move freely across the prairies, the distances they covered in a day were only as far as dogs could walk pulling heavy loads atop drag poles. That would eventually change.

The horse came, and he was such a new being that a word had to be made to describe him. He was called *sunkawakan*, or "sacred dog." It was a logical description because the horse did everything the dog did but was much larger and stronger. Everything expanded after the horse arrived, including the size of the lodge, the family inside, and the borders of Lakota territory.

The lodge that began as eight to ten feet across grew to twenty feet or more and stood as tall as thirty feet at the tops of its lodge poles. That also meant that lodge coverings had to be made larger and lodge poles had to be cut longer.

A usual day's travel of six to ten miles by foot when a camp moved became more than twenty by horse. The western boundary of Lakota territory moved from the Black Hills until it reached a line of mountains ranging north and south: the Shining Mountains, or He Wiyakpa, also known as the White Mountains, or He Ska. Those names were given because snow on the peaks gave off a shimmering or white hue when seen from a distance. Today, they are known as the Big Horn Mountains in what is now the state of Wyoming, and the Pryor Mountains in what is now Montana.

And the horse did one other thing the dog could not do: He carried people on his back.

The impact of the horse on Lakota culture is difficult to quantify. It became so much more than a beast of burden, and it was never the "work" horse that it was in other cultures. Not only was the horse well suited to the physical environment of the northern plains, it also fit in quite nicely with the established lifestyle of the Lakota.

The ability of the Lakota hunter to provide was increased exponentially, not to mention that chasing buffalo became a heart-stopping adventure. Horses with breakaway speed were chosen as "buffalo runners." After they were taught to disregard their inherent fear of buffalo—most likely because they instinctively knew that buffalo were more powerful and much faster—they were trained to pace and parallel galloping buffalo for a few precious heartbeats. This was time enough for the hunter to loose an arrow or two from a distance of ten yards or less.

Warhorses were those with calm dispositions and quick reflexes. Such horses were trained especially for close combat. They were taught to respond—like the buffalo runner—to subtle cues from the mounted warrior, such as weight shifts and leg pressure. A highly trained warhorse could drag its wounded and fallen rider out of harm's way by means of a long rope tied around its neck and looped under the arms of the warrior. Warriors composed songs to honor their horses, and like the buffalo runners, were picketed by the lodge door every night.

No, the horse did not create Lakota culture; it simply took it to levels never dreamed of. The horse was the personification of change. So, too, the Lakota themselves were the agents of change simply by crossing the east bank of the Missouri River to the west bank, and to the vast prairies beyond. And it was change that pushed the Lakota to the prairies.

The Anishinabe people, also known as the Chippewa and Ojibway, in the lake country, were enemies of the Lakota. They had traded with the French for firearms, and subsequently forced the Lakota, Dakota, and Nakota to move west from what is now Minnesota.

As the Lakota moved onto the prairie country, they displaced the Kiowa and Cheyenne. Over time, they came in contact with other people who lived on the fringes of their new territory. To the north along the Missouri were the Arikara, Mandan, and Hidatsa. Trade became the basis for a relationship with the Arikara, but the Mandan and Hidatsa were less inclined toward trade. Eventually, perhaps due to pressure from the Mandan and Hidatsa, the Arikara would often raid into Lakota territory. And they were not the only enemies.

To the northwest beyond the Black Hills lived the Bird People, known in mainstream history as the Crow. The Lakota called them Kangi Wicasa, or Crow Men. They were among their fiercest and most determined enemies.

Farther to the northwest beyond the Crow lived the Blackfeet.

Lakota contact with them was frequently with a war club, a lance, or a bow and arrow in hand. Clashes between Lakota and the Blackfeet did not happen often, however. There were more conflicts with the Shoshoni, who were in the southwestern reaches of what is now Wyoming, among the canyons and the mountains. They were also known as the Snakes and remained Lakota enemies to the last, to the point of aligning with the United States to ensure the defeat of the Lakota. About two hundred Shoshoni fighting men rode with General Crook on his push north toward the Little Bighorn in June of 1876. At the Battle of the Rosebud, they (and the Crow, who were also along) probably saved Crook from certain defeat.

There were enemies to the south as well, below the Running Water River, now known as the Niobrara, in what is now northern Nebraska. There were the Pawnee, who loved to raid north into Lakota territory for horses. Northeast of them were the Omahas, although encounters with them were infrequent.

Enemies served a purpose in Lakota culture, and indeed in most of the native cultures of the plains. All the nations shared a common lifestyle, a relationship with the same earth. As such, the Lakota understood their enemies despite their differences, and all the nations respected one another's skill, courage, and tenacity. A prevailing philosophy was that the enemy always came bearing the gift of strength, because people needed to be strong to defend themselves. To defend against an enemy, the Lakota believed that to do what was necessary to defeat him required much the same courage and mental toughness that enabled a hunter to face a grizzly bear.

Courage in the face of the enemy was a key ingredient to

victory. In addition to having the necessary skill at arms, a fighting man needed to be strong of mind and heart. This common philosophy among the plains tribes defined how warfare evolved and was conducted. But victory did not necessarily mean killing one's enemy. Victory over the mind and heart was considered to be a greater achievement. The Lakota did not fight their enemies at a distance. Instead, combat was close—very often one-on-one and intensely face-to-face, fought with hand weapons. In those arenas, the battlefield became a tangle of men and horses. With buffalo-hide shields on the left arm, warriors carried a war club or lance in the right and maneuvered their horses, working for the right opening. If the opportunity came, a warrior would simply touch or strike an opponent with his bare hand—as opposed to a killing blow or thrust with a weapon. Such an act amid the chaos of battle was considered one of the bravest deeds a warrior could perform, second only to rescuing a comrade from under the bows and guns of the enemy. Courage and strength of mind were essential.

Still, battles between enemy tribes on the northern plains did not occur as frequently as many historians believe. When they did, however, it was an opportunity for men to prove themselves. For the Lakota, demonstrating courage in the face of an enemy was the best way for a man to show himself worthy of leadership, on and off the battlefield. But engaging in combat also had a higher purpose: Warriors fought to protect their families and homes. It was considered the highest of callings and a sacred duty. Among dedicated fighting men, there was a belief that it was better to die a poor man while defending one's people than to acquire material wealth and never know the rigors of combat.

The Seven Fires

THE HORSE HELPED to establish Lakota territory by carrying the people over the next hill, across great rivers, and to the foothills of distant mountains. The Missouri River had always been the eastern border. To the south, it was the Running Water, or Niobrara River. West of there, it was the Shell, or North Platte River. The Shell turned southward at Elk Mountain (near the present town of Casper, Wyoming). North of there was the southern tip of the Big Horn, or Shining Mountains, stretching north toward the Yellowstone, or Elk River. For a short time the northwestern corner of the territory was the Powder River region, in what is now north central Wyoming. Farther east, the northern border was more or less the current North and South Dakota state border. (See map, page xix.)

By now, seven subgroups were loosely established: three large and four smaller. And they chose favorite areas as home, staying within those loose boundaries but moving freely within them.

The largest of the subbands were the Oglala, a name that means "to scatter" or "to scatter themselves." And scatter they did, over a large area from the Shell or North Platte River north to the Tongue River, in what is now central and northern Wyoming. Their western border was the Big Horn Mountains.

Second largest were the Sicangu, which means "burnt thigh." The French translation, which is often used, is Brule. They established themselves in an area that is the south central third of what is now the state of South Dakota. It is more or less a triangular area bordered on the east by the Missouri River, on the south by the Niobrara River, and on the north where the Bad River flows into the Missouri.

Next were the Hunkpapa, which means "to camp at the end." During the large summer gatherings, they established the tradition of positioning themselves at the southern end of the camp opening (formed like the letter *C*). Their territory was the northern tier west of the Missouri River below the Cedar (later Cannonball) River.

The Mniconju were called "those who plant by the water," and they were immediately south of the Hunkpapa, north and south of what is now known as the Moreau River. Both the Hunkpapa and Mniconju bands were in an area that is now north central South Dakota and south central North Dakota.

The Itazipacola, or "without bows," the Oohenunpa, or "two boilings" or "two kettles," and the Sihasapa, or "black soles" (often translated as "black feet"), were distinct but small bands. Because they numbered less than a thousand each and because they were closely related to the Hunkpapa and Mniconju, they were, for the most part, interspersed among them.

These subgroups are also referred to as Oceti Sakowin, or the Seven Fires, or the Seven Council Fires. They were one third of the entire nation, but their total population far outnumbered the Dakota and Nakota. They also controlled a larger territory. So the Titunwan scattered themselves over the vast prairie lands and guarded the exterior boundaries they had established. They were strong, but not imperialistic. They were respectful of the physical realities of their world, and on it they thrived. Their movement over the land and their connection to it is a story as old as mankind. And the Lakota thrived because they understood one basic reality: that it was easier and wiser to adapt to the land rather than to attempt to alter the land significantly to fit their needs. It was a philosophy that would eventually clash with another. But until that time, they lived, moved, danced, and watched the sun rise and set as a free people.

The gathering at the Little Bighorn occurred because the people always came together to talk about critical issues. At this particular time in Lakota history, the issue of white incursion was as serious as it could be, and it was the primary reason the people gathered. Ironically, it was the last time they would be together as a free, nomadic people. Nonetheless, the historical context within which it occurred does not overshadow what the gathering really was: an expression of cultural identity, a demonstration—and an enduring symbol—of all that the Lakota were until that pivotal summer. The identity and character of a culture that was refined and tempered by the northern plains was never more evident than that summer along the Little Bighorn, and never more connected to its beginnings.

FIVE

Grandmother

Grandmother, you who listen and hear all,
You from whom all good things come . . .
It is your embrace we feel when we return to you . . .

—from Frank Fools Crow's prayer
acknowledging the Earth

TO THE LAKOTA, the earth was alive because it was the source of life. As such it was more than a symbol for mother; she was *the* mother of everything that lived and moved. She was the epitome of generosity because she provided for all of her children. When the Lakota prayed, the earth was called Grandmother. At the Little Bighorn, Grandmother was also an ally.

There were a variety of reasons why Sitting Bull chose the area of the Little Bighorn as the eventual gathering place for that summer of 1876. Over the years, the Lakota had met there to do the Sun Dance, so there was that special connection. But given the encroachment of whites and the establishment of the Red Cloud and Spotted Tail agencies (reservations) in what is now northwest Nebraska, Sitting Bull felt that the Little Bighorn region was a reasonably safe place, beyond the easy reach of soldiers. He was, of course, unaware of the United States Army's specific plan to pursue and capture the Lakota in a three-way pincer. His goal was to bring the people together in order to talk to the influential leaders among the various bands. He wanted to talk about how best to defend themselves and their lands against further white encroachment. In a very real way, and not totally unexpected by Sitting Bull and other elders, the land itself rose up in that defense. The earth embraced the Lakota.

The gathering began to the east in the area of the Chalk Buttes—small at first, with only a few hundred. But it grew. As the days and weeks passed, more and more people came, many of them breaking away from the Red Cloud and Spotted Tail agencies. A few hundred had become a few thousand by the time they pitched their lodges near Ash Creek, a few miles from the Little Bighorn River and its wide valley.

The people who came responded to Sitting Bull's message. They wanted to hear his views on the changes forced on them by the invasion of white people. More important, they wanted to hear how he planned to mitigate the problem. They never dreamed, of course, that they would be witnesses to a pivotal time in the history of the Lakota people. They could not foresee that they would fight two battles in the span of eight days— major battles that would affect their descendants for generations to come. And the outcome of those battles, especially the last, would be dictated significantly by the land itself.

In late June of 1876, near the end of the Month When Berries Are Good, or Wipazuke Waste Wi, the great throng of thousands moved their encampment. From broken hills near Ash Creek, they hauled their lodges northeast for several miles and settled on the floodplain on the western side of the Little Bighorn, or Greasy Grass River. There was good grass for the horses there. The floodplain stretched essentially north and south for miles until the meandering stream connected with the Bighorn River, at the present town of Hardin, Montana. Lush tall grass filled the bottomland, made to order for the horse herd numbering in the thousands.

On the eastern side of the river, the land rose suddenly and formed a line of ridges that undulated sharply as they followed the river for several miles. Long slopes, deep gullies, and steep sides made the ridges formidable obstacles to easy movement, except for the likes of deer and antelope.

Within the protective canopy of young and old cottonwood groves, the people pitched their lodges, about a thousand. In length, the encampment stretched over two miles. Its northern end lay just beyond Medicine Tail Coulee, a broad gully that opened onto the river from the eastern side.

The primary reason for moving camp from Ash Creek was grass for the horses. In less than a month, the grass in that area had been grazed down considerably. If that had not happened so quickly, the camp probably would not have had to move when it did. Very possibly, the horses influenced the way the Seventh Cavalry had to approach the attack on the Little Bighorn encampment. The battle certainly would have been tactically different if the encampment had been still situated along Ash Creek. The Little Bighorn location forced Major Reno to charge north across two miles of open ground. This was not easy to do with horses exhausted from a nearly two-day forced march.

The open floodplain south of the new encampment offered scant cover. When Reno halted his charge and formed his men into a long east-west skirmish line, he lost any hope of success. In the open, without cover, Reno's troopers were susceptible to any counterattack by the Lakota and Northern Cheyenne fighters, who had an unobstructed view of the dismounted soldiers. Every fourth soldier moved to the rear with four horses, meaning that about thirty were not directly engaged in the fighting. Their main responsibility at that moment was to hold and keep control of the horses. Gall, the Hunkpapa Lakota war leader, led an attack aimed at the western end of the skirmish line, breaking it immediately with a furious charge. The soldiers fled east to where groves of trees offered cover along the river.

Most of Reno's soldiers were able to gain protective cover inside those groves. But that position also reduced their field of fire. Incoming fire was intense as the soldiers were quickly surrounded. What had seemed like a safe position for them at first had only given the Lakota and Northern Cheyenne a focused field of fire. Confused and unorganized, the soldiers finally broke from cover and retreated across the river. Here again, the terrain turned against them.

Crossing the river was the epitome of an exercise in futility. Reno's command was totally at the mercy of the warriors. One warrior later compared that specific action to "shooting ducks on the water." The river crossing offered no cover, of course, and the soldiers could do little to effectively counter incoming fire. All they could do was retreat.

Once across the river, their only choice was to climb the steep, uneven slopes in a desperate attempt to find a defensive position. Progress up the slope was slow. Soldiers and horses fell. Some three hundred yards later, in the middle of a swale on a ridge, Reno and his men were finally able to regroup and establish a defensive posture. But while the swale offered some cover, which they augmented by putting up barricades of saddles, dead horses, and crates, and digging shallow pits, the land once again aided the Lakota and Northern Cheyenne.

As the soldiers dug in, the warriors dismounted and spread out around them, taking advantage of the cover the hills and gullies offered. Now the soldiers were contained. A few attempts were made to break out of the barricades, but each was beaten back. There, for all intents and purposes, ended the Valley Fight. Reno's troopers would be reinforced by Captain Benteen returning from his foray to the south. The soldiers did improve their barricades and build rifle pits, but they were no longer a threat to the people in the large encampment across the river below. Their defensive barricaded position is now known as Reno-Benteen Hill. They would endure a long, hot night tending to their wounded. With the new day, June 26, came foot and mounted assaults against their position. Though they defended themselves well, by and large, they were contained. If scouts had not reported more soldiers to the north, the Reno-Benteen position would have been completely surrounded and sealed off as the days wore on. Once their food and water was depleted, the hot sun and the dry land would likely have sealed their fate.

While Reno was being chased to the trees, then out of the trees, then across the river, Custer was moving his five companies north behind the ridges. Though the ridges hid the movement of his column, he could not see the encampment he suspected was in the river's valley west below the ridgelines. Even after he reached a high point to have a brief look, he did not gain an accurate visual or tactical assessment of the situation below him. The groves of cottonwood obscured the camp, allowing Custer a glimpse of only a few of the thousand or so lodges, suggesting that the encampment was much smaller than it really was. Furthermore, he assumed that Reno was maintaining offensive momentum.

Custer proceeded to Medicine Tail Coulee and likely assumed that Reno had the situation well in hand. Because the trees in the floodplain hid the camp, he may have assumed that the ford at Medicine Tail Coulee would place him well past the northern end. He could cross and attack the camp. The ridges he had been using as cover prevented him from attacking at any other point into the encampment. It would have been a difficult descent, at best, down steep western slopes above the river. He would not have had the element of surprise he was so fond of. He lost it nonetheless when he decided to send a patrol across the river.

With the five companies waiting in column formation, the patrol attempted to cross the river still flowing heavily with late spring snowmelt. Defensive fire from a hidden position stopped the patrol and forced it to turn back to the east bank. Shortly thereafter, warriors led by the Hunkpapa war leader Gall crossed at or near the Medicine Tail ford.

Custer's companies by then were already urging their tired horses up a long slope, and eventually they reached the top of a plateau. That plateau connected to a north-south ridge. Custer's tired horses and the long ridge enabled Gall to close the gap easily and flank the soldiers on either side.

Historians theorize that from Medicine Tail Coulee looking west, Custer may have spotted hundreds of women and children fleeing the encampment in a northwesterly direction. He knew, of course, that noncombatants usually sought shelter away from the battle. It is possible that he intended to pursue and capture the fleeing women and children, as he had done at the Washita in 1868. However, he could not have known precisely the kind of terrain he would have to traverse before he could reach them. The long slope up from Medicine Tail Coulee was the first obstacle. The second was Gall and his fighting men in hot pursuit.

Whatever his intentions might have been, Custer had to move his troops up a long ridge. Gall's arrival probably turned Custer's offensive pursuit into a defensive action. Without substantial rest after a thirty-six-hour forced march, Custer had no choice but to gallop away from Gall's pursuing warriors. The long upward slope took its toll on the larger cavalry horses. And it enabled Gall, whose men were riding much fresher horses accustomed to the terrain, to gain the advantage.

Once on the ridge, the soldiers dismounted to form skirmish lines twice to attempt to slow or stop the advancing warriors. But in each case the incoming fire was too intense, and the lines broke. It would be the only organized defense the soldiers would muster.

The soldiers stayed on the ridge as they fled from the pursuit, honoring the age-old military precept to keep to the high ground. But having the high ground in this case did not give them any advantage, because they were flanked on either side and pursued from the rear. There was no other option for Custer's troopers but to move away from the pursuit. The only hope the soldiers might have had was a turn of luck, but it never materialized. Because they stayed to the high ground, Custer's men were easily contained with a fluid field of fire.

As the remainder of Custer's troopers approached the northern end of the ridge, a group broke off and headed west, down the slope toward the river. There is no way, of course, to know their exact motivation, or who among them took the initiative. Perhaps they thought or hoped there was cover close to the river. Several from this breakaway group were cut down almost immediately after they broke away from the ragged formation on the ridge, but over two dozen of them managed to reach a deep ravine close to the river. There they found temporary cover, but the ravine, unfortunately, was above a known river crossing, one being used by warriors attacking the left flank of the main soldier column. The flanking warriors saw the soldiers huddled in the ravine and surrounded them. Two or three rapid volleys into the ravine turned the soldiers' temporary cover into a grave. Their remains are there to this day.

Meanwhile, other soldiers reached the northern end of the ridge, at a spot now called Last Stand Hill. It is actually not a hill but the end of the ridge, and it was the end of the battle for what remained of Custer's five companies. There was simply nowhere else to go. Crazy Horse had arrived, after crossing the river to the west and below the end of the ridge. He and his warriors effectively blocked any chance for an advance farther north after he had led a devastating charge at a particularly stubborn group of soldiers. Meanwhile, more and more warriors were arriving on the scene. Gall had ordered some of his warriors, those he knew to be expert marksmen, to dismount in order to take careful aim and make good use of the limited supply of bullets they had. Using every cover the slopes offered—be it a gopher mound; a thick, bristly soapweed; or a shallow ravine—Gall's sharpshooters sniped from up to a hundred yards away. Consequently, between Crazy Horse's thunderous charge and Gall's sharpshooting riflemen, less than fifty soldiers reached the end of the ridge.

The Battle of the Little Bighorn began when Major Marcus Reno and his command of about 120 men crossed the Little Bighorn just south of its confluence with Ash Creek, and turned north. Nearly six miles north and on the opposite side of the river, the second engagement ended at Last Stand Hill. This was the length of the battlefield.

Its breadth was narrow, only about a mile at its widest point. This was the distance from the westernmost end of Reno's skirmish line to the barricade atop Reno-Benteen Hill. The second engagement was fought in a slim corridor, along what is now known as Battle Ridge, to its northern tip.

The land along the Little Bighorn where the battle was fought 130 years ago has changed little. Houses now stand where the Lakota and Northern Cheyenne were encamped. The river itself has changed its course somewhat since then, but it still meanders below the tall guardian cottonwood trees. Little Bighorn Battlefield National Monument has three hundred thousand visitors each and every year. Most are Euro-Americans, and their reactions to the story of the battle vary widely. Some walk away with nothing more than a shrug and a digital camera filled with hurried snapshots. Some are openly sympathetic to the victors. But there are those who feel and express outrage that the Seventh Cavalry was so decisively defeated. On the other hand, an overwhelming number of native people who visit the battlefield—especially Lakota and Cheyenne—feel some degree of pride.

People will continue to visit the site in the years and generations to come. Whether connected directly or not so directly to the event, most visitors will talk about the battle and all the various factors that are part of its story. And now and then, someone will say that the land itself is part of the story. It can be an emotional experience. Some will feel something emanate from the land itself. Perhaps what we seem to sense is that no one knows the complete story of that long ago battle—except the land.

And Grandmother will outlive us all.

SIX

Leading the Way

THE LITTLE BIGHORN RIVER has changed its course over the past 130 years, but it is much the same as it was on June 25, 1876. Ridges, gullies, slopes, and the flat floodplain are much the same also. Sagebrush still wafts its sweet odor, the sun still beams hot on a summer day, and the wind still blows. It is easy to perceive these connections to that battle so long ago, easy to consider how the physical and environmental factors could have been, and were, part of that event. However, there are other contributive factors that are not as evident to any visitor to the site today. One of them is leadership.

Perhaps the most common question posed by visitors to the Little Bighorn Battlefield (albeit somewhat rhetorically) is "How could this have happened?" Meaning how could the Seventh Cavalry have been so thoroughly defeated? There are, of course, many reasons why.

Leadership among the Lakota and Northern Cheyenne is an often overlooked factor. In order to understand and appreciate this attribute—more so than that the Seventh Cavalry faced superior numbers or that the victors were just plain lucky—it is essential to understand the role of leadership in Lakota culture.

Leadership existed in prereservation Lakota society in several ways, but it more or less began and ended with one group: a council of elders. Membership on the council was not by election. All elderly men of good reputation were eligible to sit as members.

The men who made up the council in any group or community had the combined experience of hundreds of years of life experience at the very least, and many of them had been military or civilian leaders. This vast resource was knowledge to bear each time any issue was brought before them. But the council had no authority to issue orders or directives that had to be followed. After the council discussed each issue at length, it offered advice on how to deal with the matter. Rarely did the people in the community, including military and civilian leaders, disregard the advice.

The council, then, was the contemplative body. The elderly men on it—by the strength of their years of experience—had become the thinkers and philosophers. The level immediately below them was a group whose responsibility was to actively lead, either in the various warrior societies or on the field of battle. If they lived long enough, they would eventually sit on the council.

Just as the members of the council were not elected, no leader was ever elected. If a man was of upstanding character and had a solid record of accomplishment, he became a leader by popular consensus; that is, the people asked him to lead. Thereafter, in order to keep his position, he had to act and make decisions always with the welfare of the people foremost in mind. There was no term of office. He was a leader as long as he was willing and able, and he did not voluntarily relinquish the responsibility unless the people ousted him.

In Lakota society, there were military and civilian leaders. In most cases, a civilian leader had first been a successful military leader, though not every military leader became a civilian leader. The system evolved over many, many generations, and it was one based on actions instead of words. The following story is a classic example of action-oriented leadership:

A group of prehistoric hunters somewhere on the Great Plains of Turtle Island have surrounded a woolly mammoth. Half a dozen men are armed with long, heavy lances. They have driven their quarry for days, not allowing it to browse or take water. The mammoth is weak, but dangerously surly.

Each hunter carries three or four lances. Each is tipped with razor-sharp fluted stone points. Thrust into a vulnerable area, such a weapon can cause severe bleeding. But the lances are primarily thrusting, not throwing, weapons. In order to do the requisite damage, the hunters must move well within the striking range of the mammoth, risking their own lives and limbs.

The strategy is simple: One or two hunters dash in close, feigning attack. When the ponderous mammoth turns to defend itself, the hunters on the other side will have a brief opening. But when the moment comes to act, fear and caution hold them back. The oldest man in the group, however, is standing back and carefully observing. He then instructs the others to lure the mammoth a short distance away, then run past a certain thicket when he charges after them. The old hunter hides in that thicket.

The other hunters follow his instructions, and the mammoth lumbers past the thicket. At the right moment, the old hunter thrusts his lance deep between the mammoth's ribs, inflicting a fatal wound. After that, another hunter manages to stab the animal, and they all continue to harass it to keep it moving. When the animal has lost too much blood, it finally topples.

Though he is nearly past his physical prime, the old hunter is experienced enough to know that luck and opportunity can be a hunter's best weapons. He has also learned to be observant, ever on the lookout for opportunity. Finally, he is courageous even though his life is in danger.

Back at camp, as everyone feasts, the other hunters tell the people the story of the hunt, having learned the value of experience. But they have also learned the necessity of having the courage and experience to act. The old hunter has taught them that. The next time a hunting party leaves camp, all the hunters fall in line behind the brave, wise old hunter.

This story of the old hunter is indicative of how leadership was earned and respected in many native cultures.

Many aspects of Lakota culture made it unique and unlike many western cultures. The idea of individual choice was one of them. Every person had free choice, as did every village or family group. For example, a war leader would announce plans to lead a scouting patrol into enemy territory and invite warriors to accompany him. But the invitation was not an order, and warriors could decide to participate or not. (The choice was based mostly on the reputation of the man leading the patrol.) Likewise, one family group might decide to move their lodges to a favorite site, and another would choose another site. The decision of warriors to join the scout was accepted by everyone, regardless of any opinion anyone had or expressed. In the same way, one family's choice to pitch their lodges wherever they wanted was respected.

Individual choice was especially critical in the selection and retention of leaders. It was a very effective counterpoint to arrogance, selfishness, brashness, and bad judgment. One's choice *not* to follow a particular leader was just as important as the choice *to* follow. Men who aspired to leadership were well aware of this factor.

There was more than one way to become a leader. A fortunate

few were born into influential families. Or a man could prove himself over time. But courage, character, and good judgment were the necessary prerequisites for leadership no matter the path to it. A young man from an influential family perhaps had some advantage because of the reputation of a father, grandfather, or an uncle. But at some point, he was also expected to demonstrate the same leadership qualities expected of anyone. If he was unable to do so, any following he might enjoy likely would not extend beyond his family.

The ultimate proving ground was warfare. A man who consistently demonstrated courage and good sense during the stress, chaos, and confusion of battle would likely do the same off the battlefield. Lakota society had long ago learned the necessity of the warrior. Life was not worth living unless you were compelled to defend it now and again, according to many elders. The defenders were the fighting men. Warriors were one of the obvious indicators of the strength of a community, or of a people. The basis for that strength was twofold: First, every male was a fighting man for most of his life. Consequently, the Lakota had a military force always available, one that could act or react instantaneously. Second, the commitment of the warrior was the unflinching defense of family and home. Being a warrior was a sacred duty, and dying in the defense of the people was the ultimate fulfillment of that duty. As a line from a warriors' honoring song says: *Oyate kin ninpi kta ca lecamu.* "I do this so that the people will live."

Within the overall brotherhood of fighting men were organizations that can only be described as warrior societies. There were various requirements for membership. To the Kangiyuha, or Crow Owners Society, a man had to have a victory (or coup) against a Crow warrior. Skayuha, or White Horse Owner, meant precisely that: A man had to own a white horse. Perhaps the most popular were the Kit Foxes, or Tokala, because the kit fox was adept at hiding and adapting to its environment. After his younger brother was killed, Crazy Horse formed a warrior society for men who had lost brothers in combat. By and large, each group had its own purpose or identity. The Bravehearts, or Cantetinzapi, and the Badgers, or Hoka, for example, were the rear guard in any action.

Each society had its own rules of conduct and officers, usually long-standing members with strong battle records. The headman was called *naca* (nah-chah), and he belonged to the *Naca Okolakiciye*, or the Headmen's Society.

The various warrior societies and the Headmen's Society were autonomous within the community at large, but they did not exist for self-fulfillment or self-perpetuation. They existed to serve and benefit the people. Because of that they were invaluable in the preparation of leaders.

But no matter how many warrior societies a man belonged to, when all was said and done, character, steadiness under pressure, and courage were the standards by which the people chose their leaders. Furthermore, it wasn't enough to simply achieve a position. A man had to understand and fulfill the responsibilities that came with it. Since legislated authority was not the means to motivate others to undertake a task and pursue an objective, leaders had only one option: They had to demonstrate leadership.

Many men who compiled enviable combat records and became military leaders had no desire for leadership as civilians. The tenure of a military leader was not an extended one, but usually coincided with his physical ability to take to the field and endure the rigors of the trail and of combat. Gall, the Hunkpapa Lakota, was such an example. A protégé of Sitting Bull, he was a formidable fighting man, standing well over six feet tall. He was a shrewd tactician and proved it at the Battle of the Little Bighorn, though, sadly, he is not given appropriate credit for his role. Later, as an older man—especially while he was in Canada with Sitting Bull and after they returned in 1881—he was the head of his family and had a following. But he never achieved the status of Sitting Bull. (Few did, of course.)

But there were those who did make the transition. The aforementioned Sitting Bull and Crazy Horse, of the Oglala Lakota, are by far the most notable.

Sitting Bull had compiled an outstanding record of achievement as a warrior. In one of his earliest battles, he suffered a serious wound to his hip, causing him to have a pronounced limp for the rest of his life. His record as a fighting man and his ability as an orator set him apart early on. He probably realized that he possessed the qualities people wanted in a leader. Therefore, when the opportunity came, he did not shy away from it. When he began to practice as a medicine man, his compassion for anyone in distress was evident. Because of his wound and his status as a healer, he became less and less active as a fighting man. But he became more valuable as a man with keen insight and the ability to assess any issue from many perspectives. Until the tragic end of his life, the Lakota people respected him for his wisdom and insight.

People flocked to Sitting Bull because he was intelligent, charismatic, and wise. During the negotiations—if they can be called that—for the 1868 treaty at Fort Laramie, he sent representatives to warn other Lakota leaders not to "touch the pen," or sign any document put forth by the white peace commissioners. In his opinion, the Lakota did not need to empower the whites or give them credibility by showing up and listening to anything they had to say. He stayed away to demonstrate his point.

In early 1875, after prospectors had infested the Black Hills and the buffalo were reduced to dangerously low numbers, Sitting Bull sent a message across Lakota country. He insisted that the white problem must be discussed and solutions found to stop the invasion into Lakota territory. The response to his message indicated the extent to which others shared his concerns, but it was also a clear statement regarding the extent of his influence as a leader. In the days after the Battle of the Rosebud, on June 17, 1876, the gathering that moved from Ash Creek to the valley of the Little Bighorn is estimated to have included between eight and ten thousand people. That number is nearly half of the entire Lakota/Dakota/Nakota nation in 1876. And most of those people broke away from the white-controlled agencies to attend the gathering. Few leaders anywhere in North America have been able to bring together a third or even a fourth of a nation under similar circumstances.

During the Ghost Dance phase of 1890, as desperation and confusion seemed to be the rule, Sitting Bull kept his counsel, wanting to learn as much as he could about Wovoka's answer to the white problem. Wovoka was the Paiute prophet who claimed to have seen a vision during a solar eclipse, a vision that showed native people how to restore the land to the way it was before the whites arrived. In order to do so, people had to perform a dance through which the dancers communed with their dead ancestors. It was called the Ghost Dance.

Interestingly, Sitting Bull never indicated that the Ghost Dance was a bad idea; he likely realized that such a pronouncement would only add to the confusion. He did say, though, that everyone had a right to decide for themselves whether to participate or not. In the meantime, he had sent a younger medicine man, Kicking Bird, to the southwest to learn about the dance from Wovoka. Kicking Bird became a believer, and he returned to inform Sitting Bull about what he had heard and seen. But his involvement as a Ghost Dance leader added a deadly dimension to the entire Ghost Dance movement.

Kicking Bird's innovation of bulletproof Ghost Shirts made the U.S. government even more nervous. There was already government fear of a widespread military uprising, especially if Sitting Bull openly endorsed the movement, because they knew of his abilities as a leader.

If there was a blot on Sitting Bull's record, in some people's minds it was his stint with Buffalo Bill's Wild West Show. It was probably the only self-indulgent thing he ever did. On the other hand, perhaps he was living up to his own philosophy that one had to know one's enemy as well as possible.

Unlike Sitting Bull, Crazy Horse was not an orator. In fact, in his life he spoke in public less than five times. Probably because the mantle of leadership was offered to him while he was still a young man, Crazy Horse was a reluctant leader.

Crazy Horse's exploits as a fighting man drew other fighting men to him. His individual achievements came early. Consequently, he became a combat leader as a very young man, reaching that status sooner than any of his predecessors. He frequently exhibited opposite sides of his persona as a warrior. On one hand, he was reckless to a fault, seemingly taunting death. On the other hand, he was capable of staying unwaveringly calm in stressful situations. Riding with him into battle, warriors knew that any man who was injured or killed would not be left on the battlefield.

Away from the battlefield, Crazy Horse was a quiet and contemplative young man. He had a lifelong habit of taking care of elderly people first. Whenever he hunted, before he took meat to his own family, he made sure the elderly had enough to eat. And he influenced others to do the same.

As a teenage boy, he had been present at the Grattan incident and had seen the aftermath of General Harney's attack on Little Thunder's village. Thereafter he understandably and steadfastly advocated resistance to white encroachment. It was clear that he was willing to stand on his convictions and take action that would ensure and defend the welfare of the people. His only stumble, as far as many Lakota are concerned, was his attempt to steal the wife of another man, never mind that she was the love of his life. His father had warned him of adverse consequences, but in a rare show of bad judgment, Crazy Horse put his own desires ahead of the welfare of the people. The entire escapade turned out badly, nearly costing him his life. In the interest of harmony among his own people, he gave up the love of his life and never again forgot his place and his responsibility.

If Crazy Horse is to be remembered for one thing and one thing only, it would have to be for his willingness to take the lead. He was always ready to set the example with action rather than direct with words. The people put their faith in him because of what he did. So they came to him willingly and often. It was not unusual for him to discover that a new family or two had quietly joined his village, sometimes during the night.

Crazy Horse and Sitting Bull were extraordinary military as

well as civilian leaders. And Crazy Horse has gone down in history as the epitome of both. But they are not isolated examples. In each of the seven Lakota divisions, there were such men. All of them are still respected, revered, and remembered by the people who knew them best. The Lakota people remember them all not because they were perfect, blameless, or never made a mistake; they remember them because of their commitment to their calling and because they did not shirk the awesome responsibility that was, in most cases, thrust upon them.

Good leaders continue to be remembered because when the time came, they lived up to their God-given abilities, and they often accomplished this in spite of their weaknesses. They understood what their community and culture expected of them. Though they experienced moments of doubt, failure now and then, and criticism and ridicule, they did their best to endure it all. Some of them—Sitting Bull, Spotted Tail, Red Cloud, Swift Bear, Crazy Horse, Touch the Clouds, and Gall—were larger than life, and their names are familiar even to people who know little or nothing of Lakota history or culture. But even the most legendary among them was as human as the least.

Interestingly, the kinds of leaders mentioned above were successful even though the Lakota language does not have a word for *authority*, as nonnative linguists and lexicographers learned in the early twentieth century. The Lakota word closest to the meaning of *authority* is *wowasake* (wo-wah-sha-keh), which means "strength" or "power." But it was and is more applicable in describing how those leaders of the past were able to lead. They did so because each man defined his position with his strength and weaknesses, his character, experience, and commitment. The position did not define him, nor did it give him power or authority. It gave him a responsibility to serve the people, not a pathway to glory or status to serve his ego.

Good leaders would find their villages growing one or a few lodges at a time. It was at once a vote of confidence and that much more responsibility. And good leaders prayed for the ability to live up to it. On the other hand, it was not at all unusual for an inept or arrogant leader to awaken on a morning and discover that his was the only lodge in the village.

Leadership, then, was a factor at the Little Bighorn. The Seventh Cavalry did not attack a village whose fighting men were inexperienced in combat, or whose military leaders did not understand tactics, or whose civilian leaders were unaware of the enormous responsibility of meeting the needs of ten thousand people. Within the ranks of the Lakota and Northern Cheyenne warriors were many leaders who were admired and respected by the men who followed them. Among the various villages and communities were elderly men whose years of experience enabled them to wield wisdom as effectively as a lance. All of those leaders were admired and respected because they had risen to the ranks of leadership by proving themselves over and over again; because they had learned from their mistakes as well as their successes.

The Battle of the Little Bighorn was not the last, or only, situation where leadership was demonstrated with action first. It happened there because that was the way leadership was defined in the Lakota culture. But this battle, perhaps more than any in the Lakota-white conflict, stands as the best example of the power of action-oriented leadership.

SEVEN

Follow Me

Hiyupo! (Follow me!)

—The first command always spoken
by Lakota war leaders

SITTING BULL, like many of his generation, watched the influx of whites into Lakota territory turn into encroachment on everyday life. It soon became an outright invasion that had killed off most of the buffalo herds on the northern plains by 1875, and more and more white miners infested the Black Hills because of the discovery of gold there. These were only some of the alarming realities that Sitting Bull wanted to change before it was too late. To do so, he had to work with the leadership hierarchy that existed among the Lakota. He had to talk to the older men who were the heads of families and villages, and to his contemporaries. That was the primary reason he issued the call for the people to gather in the spring of 1876.

None of the civilian or military leaders who were part of the great encampment of 1876 had been elected to their positions. They became leaders because of their character and their deeds. Some did not want to be leaders, but people followed them because of their good sense and good judgment. A few—like Crazy Horse, of the Oglala Lakota—were leaders both on and off the battlefield. Touch the Clouds, of the Mniconju Lakota, was another.

While Sitting Bull and other elder statesmen were busy convening councils to talk about stopping the white invasion, warrior leaders like Crazy Horse sent scouts in all directions—eyes and ears that would see any enemy that might threaten the people in the great gathering. But the war leaders did not meet night after night, day after day, as the elders did. Crazy Horse, the most esteemed of all war leaders, could have called for a gathering among all war leaders. Yet it was not necessary to make plans or train fighting men for a specific mission because all the war leaders were hardened combat veterans, having fought against many enemies, including the Long Knives. Furthermore, they knew that the skills and abilities of the fighting men allowed them to adapt to any situation they might encounter. For all of those reasons, the U.S. Seventh Cavalry could not have picked a more pivotal moment to attack the encampment.

In the encampment were about twelve hundred fighting men, most of them seasoned by combat and rested from their encounter with General Crook at Rosebud Creek only eight days earlier—an encounter they felt was a victory. Initially, less than a hundred warriors responded after the first alarms were raised as Reno's men were urging their stumbling horses across the open ground toward the southern end of the camp. Some were on foot and many were mounted; all were armed and angry. Some of the first leaders to arrive on the scene were Gall and Black Moon of the Hunkpapa Lakota, and Crazy Horse and Big Road of the Oglala Lakota. By then, the soldiers had dismounted and formed an east-west skirmish line, firing from standing, kneeling, and prone positions. Unknown to the other leaders, Gall was carrying a burden much heavier than the responsibilities of leading men into combat.

Gall was Crazy Horse's contemporary and a favorite of Sitting Bull. He was a tall, robust, and handsome man. His role in the second engagement of the Battle of the Little Bighorn (yet to come at this moment in the chronology of the battle) was the primary reason for the utter defeat of Custer's five companies. Gall's extremely critical role has long been overshadowed by the larger-than-life presence of Crazy Horse and Sitting Bull. But it is Gall, just as much as Crazy Horse, who should be credited for the overall victory at Little Bighorn.

Gall had two wives, and they, and some of their children, were at home when Reno's troopers opened fire with their .54-caliber rifles. Many of the bullets carried far into the Hunkpapa encampment at the southern end. Both of Gall's wives and one of his daughters were killed. He had been elsewhere when he heard the firing and the alarms. Hurrying home to gather his weapons, he discovered the bodies of his family.

After he carried the three bodies into his home, Gall joined the warriors who were hurrying to meet and mitigate the threat. He told no one of his heart-wrenching loss until later that evening. With Crazy Horse and the other leaders, he assessed the soldiers' skirmish line. They could all see that at the western end of the line were most of the Seventh's Indian scouts. Gall and the others knew that if that end of the line collapsed, the entire formation would be vulnerable.

Gall more or less volunteered to lead a charge, and he did so with a vengeance. He was seen in the midst of the action as scores of mounted warriors routed the soldiers. Later, when word came that soldiers had been seen on the ridges above the camp, he broke away from the Reno-Benteen siege and raced down to the valley. Crossing the meandering river more than once, he gathered warriors to him and led them to the Medicine Tail ford. There they saw a column of soldiers moving away to the northeast and up a long slope. Behind them was a small group of hard-riding Lakota warriors led by a man named Crow King.

Once across, Gall sent flankers to the right and left, a tactic that prevented the soldiers from turning back toward the river. He and his men noticed immediately that the soldiers' horses stumbled frequently up the long slope. Gall had his men fire sporadically to save precious bullets, but also to let the soldiers know they were being pursued. Near the top of the slope, they closed the gap considerably and merged with Crow King and his men, and managed to scatter a squad of soldiers that had dismounted and formed a skirmish line to fire at the oncoming warriors. The sight of mounted warriors bearing down apparently unnerved the soldiers. A few of them fled on foot, and it was here that Gall's warriors inflicted their first casualties.

Farther along the ridge, more soldiers attempted another skirmish line. Gall selected several warriors to dismount and take deliberate aim from cover. Accurate incoming fire from those hidden warriors, and more warriors gaining the ridge, quickly eliminated the second soldiers' skirmish line. It was clear now that the soldiers were disorganized, unable to return fire consistently and not taking steady aim when they did. Gall saw the effect of the steady marksmanship of his dismounted warriors, and he urged others to do the same, especially several he knew to be expert riflemen. The effect was almost immediate. Soldiers fell in a relentless rhythm. They ran and fell, ran and fell.

The Northern Cheyenne had chosen an area just north and across from the Medicine Tail crossing. From their lodges they had a good view of the wide coulee across the river that stretched to the east. Because they were over two miles from the southern end, they did not hear the soldiers open fire at the Hunkpapa end of the camp. The alarm flowed quickly from south to north, however. By the time the news reached the Cheyenne lodges, Reno's attack had already bogged down, and he was running for the river. Two Moons, the ranking civilian and military leader among the Northern Cheyenne, heard the news and urged Cheyenne warriors to go to the aid of their Lakota friends. With a knot of warriors behind him, Two Moons rode south to join the fight.

Several Cheyenne had been catching their warhorses and returned to the camp to make preparations, unaware that Two Moons and several warriors had ridden off. Before preparations were completed, someone spotted soldiers across the river at the ford. A man named Bobtail Horse was one of the warriors. He called out to his comrades, urging them to meet the threat. Only a few fighting men were left in the Cheyenne camp; nevertheless, they rode out together, one or two singing their death songs. Near the crossing they came upon several Lakota boys and old men hiding in the brush, armed and ready to fight.

As a few soldiers reached the river's edge and began to cross, the Cheyenne-Lakota contingent opened fire, forcing the soldiers to retreat. Soon thereafter the entire column of soldiers started up a long slope east of the crossing. A moment later, a

small group of Lakota (Crow King's men) crossed and chased after the departing Long Knives. Not long after that, dozens more
Lakota warriors splashed across at the ford and began to pursue
the soldiers as well. Bobtail Horse and the other Cheyenne with
him crossed and joined the pursuit.

Crazy Horse had received word of a new threat to the other end of
the camp at about the same moment as Gall. He disengaged from
the siege of the Reno-Benteen position and crossed the river, hurrying through the melee and confusion of the encampment and
calling out to warriors as he went, urging them to go north. At his
own lodge in the Oglala camp just below the Cheyennes, he took
a fresh warhorse from his wife. In the Cheyenne camp, he received
word that soldiers were being chased up the hill across the river.
Realizing that he had nearly a hundred men with him, Crazy
Horse headed for an old crossing farther downstream. He was
joined by Two Moons and several of his Northern Cheyenne warriors. At a point northwest of where the Little Bighorn Battlefield
National Monument visitor center now stands, he crossed the
river and circled east. As they reached the broken hills and gullies,
they met a surprised group of soldiers, perhaps twenty, who beat a
hasty retreat back to the south.

From a rise they heard the gunfire. The soldiers were on a long
ridge and moving northward, some of them on foot. Loose horses
were everywhere. As they rode closer to the action, it was clear the
soldiers were fighting a running battle, and losing. One group,
however, seemed to be holding their own, staying together and returning shot for shot at the advancing warriors. Crazy Horse circled farther to the east and then turned south and charged that

troublesome group. With his warriors behind him, they were able to inflict casualties and scatter the stubborn knot of soldiers.*

In leading this particular charge, Crazy Horse demonstrated the utter selflessness for which he was known. In apparent disregard for his own safety, he raced his horse at the soldiers, firing as he rode. Many of the warriors with him were awed by his actions, briefly watching the spectacular display of courage before they joined him.

Crazy Horse's act of tremendous courage combined with Gall's steady leadership contributed to the defeat of Custer and his entire command of 227 men. But on this day, other lesser-known battle leaders also lent a hand to the victory. The Hunkpapa Lakota Crow King and a few of his warriors had been the first to reach Medicine Tail Coulee, and were the first to pursue Custer's five companies up the long slope. Black Moon, another Hunkpapa Lakota, was prominent in the Valley Fight, as were Good Weasel and Good Road, both Oglala Lakota.

All these men, as well as others who led in the battle, had seen combat many times before. They were not new to the unfettered violence, noise, chaos, and confusion. They were no strangers to death, always ready to give their last full measure of devotion in order that the people would live. Some were more reckless in battle, as Crazy Horse often was; others were more steady and deliberate, as was Gall. But whatever their individual tendencies, they were all leaders.

Lakota war leaders did not stay out of harm's way and direct others. They were in the thick of it, leading the way. They will be

---

*Probably I Company, under the command of Captain Miles Keogh.

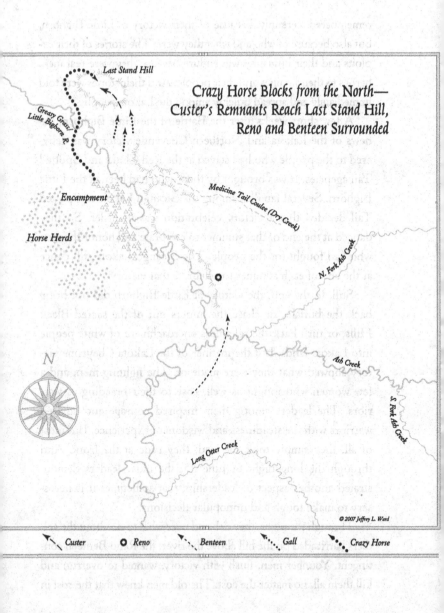

Last Stand Hill

Greasy Grass/
Little Bighorn R.

Crazy Horse Blocks from the North—
Custer's Remnants Reach Last Stand Hill,
Reno and Benteen Surrounded

Encampment

Medicine Tail Coulee (Dry Creek)

Horse Herds

N. Fork Ash Creek

Ash Creek

N

S. Fork Ash Creek

Long Otter Creek

© 2007 Jeffrey L. Ward

Custer   O Reno   Benteen   Gall   Crazy Horse

remembered, certainly, because of their victory at Little Bighorn, but also because of who and what they were. The stories of their exploits and their humanity will endure because they were real men, heroes to their families and their people. And their stories were told immediately and spread quickly among the Lakota people.

A few short weeks after the Battle of the Little Bighorn, the news of the Lakota and Northern Cheyenne victory was delivered to the people who had stayed at the Red Cloud and Spotted Tail agencies. It was brought by those who had been at the Little Bighorn. Several families among the Sicangu Lakota at Spotted Tail decided that a victory celebration was in order. So they danced at the end of that summer to celebrate and honor the men who had fought for the people. The Sicangu Lakota still dance at the end of each summer to celebrate that victory.

Still, in the end, the victory at Little Bighorn did not bring back the buffalo, or chase the miners out of the sacred Black Hills, or turn back the relentless encroachment of white people into Lakota lands. But the manner of the Lakota-Cheyenne victory showed what they were made of. The fighting men, and a few women who fought as well, rose to their breeding as warriors. The leaders among them inspired courage and advised warriors with the steadiness and wisdom of experience. But most of all, they simply took the lead; they rode at the front. And through the long night of June 25, the older leaders demonstrated another aspect of leadership: that sometimes it is necessary to make tough and unpopular decisions.

Through the night, they debated over what to do about the soldiers barricaded on the hill above the river: the Reno-Benteen contingent. Younger men, flush with victory, wanted to overrun and kill them all, no matter the cost. The old men knew that the cost in lives would be high if the younger men had their way. Nonetheless, some of the older men were in favor of the idea of killing all the soldiers. But in the night, word came, brought by scouts returning from the north beyond the Bighorn River. More soldiers were approaching.

The news immediately raised concerns over the safety of the encampment. Every man, young or old, wanted his family to be safe. Nevertheless, as the sun rose on the twenty-sixth of June, the fighting on the hill erupted. Mounted charges were met with vigorous fire. Warriors tried slipping in close, but they were pinned down. So the old men, out of concern for their women and children as well as the fighting men, decided to spare the soldiers on the hill.

The warriors withdrew, leaving a few to keep the troopers pinned down. Meanwhile, in the valley below, the women took down their lodges and packed their households. By late afternoon, the camp was moving in a long column formation, with warriors riding on the outskirts as the first line of defense.

The soldiers could do nothing but watch, likely with a certain sense of relief. Although the primary reason the camp was moving away was concern for the safety of the women and children, the soldiers were nonetheless the beneficiaries of the compassion of the old men leaders.

Across Lakota country there are families descended from the people who were at the Little Bighorn in June of 1876. The same is true of the Northern Cheyenne. Those families know who their ancestors were and what they did in the battle. Some are descendants of the men who were killed or later died of their wounds. There is no absence of pride in those families, and no absence of sadness. And they tell the stories of their ancestors to each new generation of their family. In a real sense, therefore, those warriors who fought at the Little Bighorn have gained immortality. They live on in the stories as each new generation learns who they were, and what they did, and how they lived.

Say the name Little Bighorn and one of the immediate reactions is to think of a battle. Many names are connected to the Battle of the Little Bighorn: Custer, Reno, Benteen, Keogh, Curly, Whiteman Runs Him, and Bloody Knife on one side. Sitting Bull, Crazy Horse, Gall, Black Moon, He Dog, Crow King, Good Weasel, Big Road, Two Moons, Wooden Leg, and Bobtail Horse on the other. Of course, there are many more. All of them were compelled to act because they were following orders or because they felt a sense of duty. They made a commitment, sometimes reluctantly and sometimes freely, to put themselves in harm's way.

On one side were nearly 650. On the other, somewhere between 1,200 and 1,500. Victory favored the defenders, as we all know. How that victory came to be will be debated—endlessly. Was it because of weaponry, or superior numbers, or just plain luck?

The Little Bighorn River still flows, the ridges still guard the floodplain, the sun rises and sets, and the winds still flow over the land where a battle was fought. Those are the tangible aspects of memory, as are weaponry and superior numbers. Less tangible is luck, good or bad. Even less so are the hearts and minds, the souls, and the character of the people who fought there. If the intangible is examined, some interesting insights will unfold—and perhaps some unexpected lessons will be learned. One of those lessons might be the depth of commitment and the level of inspiration in the deceptively simple phrase "Follow me!"

EIGHT

Zuya Wicasa (The Warriors)

A warrior I have been.
I have had a hard time.

—Sitting Bull, Hunkpapa Lakota

LAKOTA MALES were bred to fulfill two broad societal roles simultaneously: the hunter/warrior, or the provider/protector. These duties were not performed, however, to the exclusion or diminishment of other roles and responsibilities. Furthermore, contrary to long-held beliefs, the Lakota male did not live for war.

The word *warrior* has long been associated with native North American males, especially of the Plains tribes. (Other labels commonly used are tribesmen, braves, or the ever-popular hostiles.) Being a warrior was a necessary and critical societal role, and it was the predominant one. For many tribes like the Lakota, military service was not an obligation fulfilled with a tour of a few years. Nor was it regarded as a job or a career. Rather, military service was a lifelong calling, fulfilled in conjunction with all the other responsibilities expected of males.

The other critical responsibility was as the hunter. As a hunter, a man provided a living for his family and community.

The equipment, skills, and abilities necessary for being both a hunter and warrior were interchangeable, most notably in the area of weaponry. Although some weapons were similar in appearance, there was a definite distinction in usage because the design and configuration of a hunting weapon differed from one used for war. For example, except when it was absolutely necessary, a bow used for hunting was not used in battle, and it was the same for arrows. In the case of lances, the lance used to hunt buffalo was often twice as long as a war lance, which was rarely longer than the height of its owner.

On the other hand, some weapons were meant only for hunting, such as the throwing stick (also called a rabbit stick) used to bring down small game, and the sling for throwing stones, also used for small game. Likewise, war clubs were used only in combat. Firearms became the preferred weapons, especially for warfare, when they came on the scene.

But there was more to the hunter/warrior than his weapons. He was trained to be at home in the natural environment, in any terrain and in any weather in all seasons of the year. From about the age of five, boys were taught the skills necessary to be hunters and warriors, such as tracking, hand-crafting tools and weapons, close combat, proficiency with weapons, and horsemanship. They were mentored one-on-one by older males— fathers, uncles, grandfathers, family friends—until about the age of sixteen or seventeen. They were taken on hunts and military expeditions to observe experienced, full-fledged hunters and fighting in the field. By their late teens, Lakota males were ready to fulfill their roles and take their places as hunters and warriors.

The gender role philosophy of Lakota culture and its practical application enabled the availability of a ready fighting force.

A man never stopped being a warrior, although that role shifted around the age of fifty. Then a man no longer had the physical capabilities of younger men. So while younger men took to the field on raids and scouting missions, older men stayed in camp as the first line of defense for the women, children, and elderly. Furthermore, every fighting man was taught that his commitment as the warrior ended only with death, whether it came on the field of battle or with old age. Dying in the defense of family and home, however, was the highest of honors and the strongest legacy to leave behind. It was this kind of fighting man that the Seventh Cavalry faced in the valley of the Little Bighorn.

The six-legged warrior

ONE OF THE BIGGEST FACTORS in the Lakota victory at the Battle of the Little Bighorn was the horse. It was often said that a Lakota male had six legs: two of his own and the four belonging to his horse. This, of course, speaks to the way the horse so readily became part of the nomadic, hunting lifestyle of the Plains peoples. All native societies eventually acquired the horse, but their basic culture and lifestyle did not change. Rather, the nomadic peoples of the plains became even more nomadic. The horse did not motivate the people to move over the land. It did, however, greatly increase their mobility. Just as important, it gave the Lakota fighting man another dimension as a warrior. He became a *mounted* warrior.

Initially, the horse displaced the dog as beast of burden. He was much, much larger and stronger and therefore the loads he carried were larger. *Sunka wakan* was the label applied by the Lakota to this new and wonderful creature, *sunka* being the word for dog. The label has been translated as "sacred dog" and "holy dog," which are essentially appropriate descriptors. But for *wakan* there is no suitable word in English.

Lakota linguists do not agree on the best translation to English. "Holy" and "sacred" are close, but *wakan* can also mean "powerful," "beyond," or "greater than." For example, if a man or a woman did something extraordinary, or beyond the norm, it would be described as a "powerful act" that would be *wakan woecun*. Therefore, the Lakota label for the horse accurately described it in two ways: First, it was obviously far greater than the dog, and second, its contribution to Lakota society was beyond measure. With the horse, the Lakota expanded their population and their territories, and they fielded some of the best light cavalry the world has ever known.

The warhorses that Lakota fighting men rode into battle were picked for their temperament, endurance, and agility. They were schooled for years to respond to the rider's cues of weight shift, leg pressure, and voice. And like the warrior himself, the horse that had experienced combat was a thoroughly valuable asset. Many Lakota warriors had more than one, and sometimes they had one or two more in the process of being trained.

At dawn on the twenty-fifth of June, scouts of the Seventh Cavalry were training their field glasses to the west from a high knoll called the Crow's Nest. They saw no dwellings, only something on the floodplain west of the Little Bighorn River that resembled maggots in the grass. They saw horses, thousands of them.

Grazing peacefully on that fateful morning were the horses that formed one of the single largest herds to occupy one area, horses that belonged to the thousand or so families that were part of the Little Bighorn encampment of Lakota and Northern Cheyenne. Many were travois horses that pulled drag poles to transport household belongings and people who could no longer ride (many of these were big American horses taken on raids). There were everyday riding horses owned by each family: those belonging to boys and young men, the hunter/warriors in training, and more than a few warhorses. On the average, each family owned ten to fifteen horses.

These were the maggots in the grass, a herd probably of between twelve thousand to fifteen thousand head.

Without a doubt, the scouts knew that the horses in the valley of the Little Bighorn meant the presence of many, many people. They also knew that inside the encampment—what they could not see—were the "six-legged warriors," the fighting men and their warhorses. Customarily, the best and most valuable warhorses were picketed at their owner's lodge door, a safeguard against theft from enemy raiders.

The six-legged warrior was the single most important factor in the defeat of the soldiers at the Little Bighorn. Boys (as well as many girls) were put on a horse at the age of four or five. By the time they were twelve, they were more than adequate riders, and by the age of sixteen they had reached the level of expert. At that point, riding a horse was second nature. The basics of riding had become rather like breathing or blinking: They were done without conscious thought.

The fighting man and his horse had an emotional bond that was an intangible and fearsome weapon. When an expert rider is paired with an extremely well-trained horse, the result is a formidable instrument of warfare. Major Reno's soldiers learned that firsthand. Relentless charges by Lakota horsemen broke the soldiers' skirmish line and turned Reno's attack into a Lakota rout. The second engagement of the battle began with a pursuit of Custer's five companies up the slope away from Medicine Tail Coulee (or Dry Creek). Gall led his men across the river and charged after the fleeing soldiers. That engagement ended at Last Stand Hill after a relentless chase. Part of the reason for this outcome was the Seventh Cavalry's worn-out horses and the fresher mounts of the Lakota and Northern Cheyenne. But the larger reason was the skill and daring of the six-legged warriors.

In a heartbeat

IN THE 1950s and 1960s, Lakota and Cheyenne schoolchildren were taught the story of the colonial minutemen. They were ordinary men who farmed and followed other pursuits of the day, but they also kept their muskets and powder horns at hand in order to respond at a minute's notice to the ever-present threat from the British army.

Native societies across North America had invented this strategy long before the American colonies were established. Non-Indian teachers who extolled the courage of the minutemen probably did not realize that the Lakota children in their classrooms learning about the American Revolution were two and three generations removed from ancestors who had employed this tactic in their fight for freedom.

Every day (except in extremely inclement weather), in every encampment large or small during any season of the year, near the lodge doors were reassuring reminders of the strength of the community. On a tripod of willows to the left or right of the door were attached the weapons and accoutrements of the warrior (or warriors) who lived in the lodge. If the tripod was bare, it meant that the warrior was away.

Weapons and accoutrements arranged in such a manner were practical as well as symbolic. When the fighting man was at home in the encampment, he knew where his weapons were and could grab them in an instant if necessary. Such a display also demonstrated that the fighting men of the community were ready to rise to the defense of the people in a heartbeat.

Nothing succeeds like success

THE SOLDIERS who attacked the encampment on the Little Bighorn were unaware that eight days earlier, several hundred Lakota fighting men and their Northern Cheyenne allies had stopped General George Crook's northern advance fifty miles to the south. As a matter of fact, they had carried the fight to Crook at Rosebud Creek (just north of the present town of Sheridan, Wyoming).

In a real sense, the Battle of the Little Bighorn and the Battle of the Rosebud were two separate events. But the outcome at the Rosebud bolstered the confidence of the Lakota and Northern Cheyenne—not to mention that it also provided valuable experience. Yet the Battle of the Rosebud is rarely considered a factor in the outcome of the Battle of the Little Bighorn.

When the first shots opened the Rosebud battle at dawn on the seventeenth of June, Crook's soldiers and their Crow and Shoshoni allies were waking from a night's rest. For their part, the attacking force led by Crazy Horse had just completed a *fifty-mile ride in the dark.* Without any rest, they engaged the enemy in a battle that ended in the late afternoon. When Crazy

Horse decided to withdraw his fighters from the field, Crook did not have the means to stop him. Subsequently, the Lakota and Northern Cheyenne rode the *fifty miles back* to their encampment, which was near Ash Creek at the time, arriving at dawn after nearly thirty-six hours without significant rest.

Crazy Horse and his battlefield leaders and fighting men had engaged a numerically superior force that had more guns and ammunition. For all intents and purposes, the battle was probably a draw. But because Crook could do no more than lick his wounds and withdraw to the south, the Lakota considered it a victory. What they did not know was that they had effectively dismantled the U.S. Army's grand plan to catch them in a trap. Crook had been one third of that plan. Eight days later they spoiled the trap entirely after Lieutenant Colonel George Custer ordered the Seventh to attack, prematurely, as it turns out.

Little Bighorn still would have been a victory for the Lakota if Rosebud had not occurred, simply because there were too many factors in their favor. But confidence bolstered by the outcome at Rosebud Creek was an immeasurable advantage. When Lakota fighting men realized that the Little Bighorn encampment was under a full-scale attack, many of them thought it was the soldiers from the Rosebud fight seeking revenge. A recurring thought must have gone through many of their minds: We did it once and we can do it again.

A vision fulfilled

A FEW SHORT WEEKS before the Battle of the Rosebud, while the people were still encamped along Ash Creek, Sitting Bull had conducted a Sun Dance and been given a vision. He had seen soldiers and their horses falling from the sky, their ears cut off. They were falling into a circle of Lakota lodges.

Soldiers falling into camp became a prediction of victory, and many were quick to say that Sitting Bull's vision had been fulfilled at the Rosebud. But many elders were just as quick to disagree, because Crazy Horse had carried the battle to the soldiers. There were those who felt strongly that the Hunkpapa holy man's vision had yet to be realized. And in the first moments when gunfire blasted the stillness of a lazy afternoon on the twenty-fifth of June, many people were filled with apprehension when it became apparent that an attack was under way. But at the same time, many remembered Sitting Bull's vision, even as they prepared for battle or grabbed their children and elderly to flee from the soldiers.

Sitting Bull himself exhorted warriors to have courage and remember the helpless ones, but not because he was uncertain of the outcome of the developing battle. He shouted encouragement because he knew that the courage of warriors was key to fulfilling his vision.

Sitting Bull was at the height of his influence and power as a holy man. He had been a formidable warrior in his younger days and had won nearly seventy war honors. For that record of achievement, he had the respect of every fighting man in the encampment. To them, his vision was a guarantee of victory.

No one was foolish enough to think that fighting the soldiers would be easy. The threat had to be confronted, and so it was. No one had to remind any fighting man of the dire consequences if the soldiers were to gain the advantage. It was common knowledge that soldiers killed and mutilated women and children, but they were also the symbol and the instrument of white invasion into Lakota lands and life. Everything that every fighting man held near and dear was in that encampment, and every man was willing to lay down his life to defend it.

Early in the first attack, the Valley Fight, Sitting Bull's vision literally came true. Before Major Reno dismounted his men and formed a skirmish line, at least two, perhaps three, soldiers were carried into the encampment by their mounts. The horses, probably frightened and confused by the chaos and gunfire, could not be controlled. Inside the camp, the soldiers were caught, and pulled down and killed. After the last engagement of the day ended and warriors heard of the incident, many were not surprised. That incident was an affirmation of the power of Sitting Bull's vision.

Some say that the Lakota fighting man had his finest day at the Little Bighorn, but such an opinion is often expressed without full knowledge of the conflicts faced by the Lakota. Many of the Little Bighorn warriors were at least thirty-five years of age and had seen considerable fighting. There had been at least five major battles against the U.S. Army during the 1860s, not to mention the fighting along the Bozeman Trail against white civilians. Furthermore, many had fought against the Crow and the Shoshoni, long-standing and staunch enemies.

Most of those who fought at Little Bighorn would likely agree that the three engagements over two days of fighting were some of the hardest fighting they had experienced. But not all would agree that it was their finest day, based partially on their opinion of their opponents. To some fighting men, soldiers were not honorable enemies. To defeat them was necessary, to be sure. If any man felt that the victory there was a "fine" achievement, that feeling was primarily because the warriors had successfully defended the people. And that, after all was said and done, was what a Lakota warrior was committed to doing.

The Lakota fighters who rose to meet the enemy that day on the Little Bighorn, the Greasy Grass to them, were ordinary men. They were husbands, fathers, sons, grandsons, and grandfathers. They would still be heroes to us, the Lakota of today, even if they had lost the battle. They are heroes because they defended their own. By doing so, they did what men in any culture or society have done throughout the ages. They were not supermen, but pound for pound, they were better trained and more highly skilled as fighters than the soldiers they faced that day.

The Lakota words for warrior are *zuya wicasa* (zoo-yah we-chah-shah), literally meaning "war man," but also translated as "man who goes to war." *Zuya* means "war" and *wicasa* means "man."

During each generation, many Lakota families pass down the story of ancestors who fought at the Little Bighorn. Though they did not live for war, neither did they turn away from it. Their legacy as warriors will live on, therefore, as reminders, as examples, and as inspiration. Those fighting men—those real warriors—will always be heroes.

NINE

The Long Knives

MILA HANSKE, they were called. Long Knives. One of the distinctive features immediately noticed by the first Lakota to see soldiers of the U.S. Army was the sword. So the name stuck.

The word *akicita* is now used for soldier. Lakota people use the word in reference to the nineteenth-century soldier, but it was not initially applied until after the turn of the twentieth century. Among prereservation Lakota warrior societies, the *akicita* were the men charged with keeping order when camps relocated, or during buffalo hunts. After Lakota young men joined the U.S. Army and served during World War I, *akicita* became "soldier." It was the Lakota word that came closest to describing what the soldier did. Today when young Lakota people join any branch of the U.S. military, their families say *akicita opapi*, or "they have joined the soldiers."

But in 1876 the soldiers were *mila hanska*. Most Lakota felt the only thing good about them was their weapons, and the worst thing was that they simply would not go away. They were rightfully perceived to be instruments of the Great Father and of the peace talkers. The president of the United States was given the title of Great Father by the peace commissioners, or peace talkers, the representatives of the U.S. government sent to negotiate with native tribes. In this hierarchy, the soldiers were the people sent to enforce the will of the Great Father and his peace talkers, or inflict punishment if the Lakota and other tribes had done something wrong.

The Lakota and Northern Cheyenne faced, in battle, some 1,600 soldiers that summer of 1876, not to mention the 300 Crow and Shoshoni who rode with General Crook and 50 scouts with Custer. They fought Crook's force of 1,300 to a standstill on June seventeenth and manhandled Custer's 650 men on the twenty-fifth.

As far as the Lakota were concerned, two factors were always constant with the soldiers: One, they fought to kill and killed indiscriminately; and two, they were always well armed with plenty of ammunition and often had "wagon guns," a field cannon or howitzer.

On that hot June day, the soldiers' intentions and orders were to ride into the encampment where the women and children were. This is not hard to believe, considering Custer's and his regiment's attitude toward noncombatants. In fact, General Philip Sheridan once described George Custer, the commander of the Seventh, as a "man who wept with his wife at sentimental drama but [who] could ride whooping with his troops over an Indian village full of women and children."

So when Custer arrived at the ford at Medicine Tail Coulee, hundreds of women and children were in full flight, strung out on the floodplain to the northwest across the river. They would have been easy to spot from Medicine Tail Coulee. Custer did proceed north from the coulee, perhaps with the intention of circling back to the west to cut off and capture the fleeing women and children. But his truest intentions will never be known because Lakota warriors crossed the ford and pursued him, forcing him to run and fight simultaneously.

At about the same time that Custer and his five companies were being pursued up and away from Medicine Tail Coulee, Major Marcus Reno, second in command of the Seventh Cavalry, and the remnants of his companies were digging in on a ridge overlooking the river, three miles to the south. Captain Frederick Benteen, one of the Seventh's senior company commanders, was returning from his reconnaissance to the south, and was about to join Reno. (Neither Major Reno nor Captain Benteen were favorites of Custer's.) On that ridge, about 375 soldiers, including those with the pack train, became tactically ineffective. Like Custer and his five companies, they would be reduced to basic survival mode.

The Seventh Cavalry was formed by the U.S. Army in 1866 and headquartered at Fort Riley, in Kansas. Most of the senior officers, such as Reno and Benteen, were with the regiment almost from the beginning. The regiment's main duty seemed to be harassing tribes on the southern plains. An incident in late November of 1868 on the Washita River, in what is now Kansas, known as the Battle of the Washita, set the tone for the Seventh Cavalry's purpose. The regiment attacked Black Kettle's Southern Cheyenne village at dawn while most of the men were away. In addition to combatants, they killed women and children and took captives, a stellar achievement in the eyes of the army perhaps, but regarded as a cowardly act by most of the southern plains tribes.

Overall, the Seventh's stint in the southern plains region was unspectacular, but the regiment was assigned other duty as well. From 1871 to 1873 and again from 1874 to 1876, several of the Seventh's companies were sent to the Reconstruction South to do what was called constabulary duties.

Throughout the Seventh Cavalry's early years, it was plagued with desertions—sometimes as high as 50 percent. The glory of being "Indian fighters" alone was apparently not enough to keep soldiers in the field. The problem angered Lieutenant Colonel George Custer to the point that he ordered deserters shot. (Interestingly, Custer himself was suspended from duty for a year for being AWOL—absent without leave.)

In 1873, the regiment was reassigned to Fort Abraham Lincoln in Dakota Territory, across the Missouri River from the present state capital of Bismarck, North Dakota. Prior to their arrival, Fort Abraham Lincoln was an infantry post, but their units had difficulty matching the Hunkpapa Lakota. The well-mounted Hunkpapa, as it turned out, were much too mobile for the infantry companies. So continued requests from the post commander for a cavalry unit eventually brought the Seventh to the northern plains. And in early August of that year, they met their future foes.

The Seventh was assigned to escort a survey expedition laying out a route for a railroad, mainly through what is now eastern Montana. West of the present town of Miles City, the escort party clashed with Oglala, Hunkpapa, and Mniconju warriors led by Crazy Horse. This was the first encounter between Crazy Horse and the Seventh Cavalry. Neither side, however, inflicted significant casualties on the other.

The following year, the regiment became more of a threat to the Lakota when it was dispatched to the Black Hills to confirm the rumors of the discovery of gold.

The posting at Fort Abraham Lincoln would, of course, make them part of the U.S. Army's plan to capture the defiant Lakota in the summer of 1876. On May 17, they marched out of

Fort Abraham Lincoln as part of a larger force commanded by General Alfred E. Terry.

Most of the men of the Seventh Cavalry probably had never seen Plains Indians until they enlisted, or until their posting at Fort Abraham Lincoln, although some of them had seen service in the Civil War. Within the Seventh's ranks, nearly twenty European languages were spoken. Many of the men were not American citizens, and at least three were part native. The average age was mid to late twenties. Because the army preferred smaller men for the cavalry, most of the Seventh's soldiers were between five feet three inches and five feet eight inches tall. U.S. Army records indicate fewer than six men who were six feet tall or over. Of course, part of the Seventh's roster included the scouts, fifty-one in all, from at least six different tribes.

The regiment was—perhaps more so in retrospect—styled as an elite fighting force. Yet at the time, army budgetary constraints severely limited target practice for soldiers in the field. Another bothersome factor would prove just as costly later: The army-issued copper cartridge casings for the Springfield rifle frequently cracked after repeated firing and jammed in the breech, which made reloading difficult. As a result, many officers purchased their own ammunition. This was, apparently, only one of the liabilities the Seventh carried into the field in the summer of 1876.

General Terry was in overall command at Fort Abraham Lincoln. The Seventh was easily half of that command, which included three companies of infantry and nearly two hundred civilians employed by the army. As long as the terrain and weather conditions were favorable to large troop movement, the Seventh was highly mobile. On the whole, American troops posted on the northern plains were formidable when operating at large-unit strength, primarily because of their firepower. (Two Gatling guns were part of the ordnance Terry took into the field.)

Conventional military units depend on unit cohesion and the ability of each of their subgroups to function adequately. Further, unit cohesion must depend on several factors, chief among them the ability of the unit commander—be it the company commander or squad leader—to maintain command and control, and the ability of the individual soldier to perform well in the midst of chaos, confusion, and fear. If the unit commander does not quickly evaluate the tactical situation at hand or gain effective control of it, the consequences can be disastrous.

To this end, soldiers were trained to function as a unit under the authority of one unit leader or commander. If leadership was not exercised, or exercised poorly, or eliminated by the enemy, the unit lost its cohesion. If the next in line did not assume command, unit cohesion could have been lost permanently. The final opportunity to prevent total disorganization then rested on each individual soldier, and how that soldier performed depended on the training he had received as well as the depth of his character and courage.

Despite their often heinous behavior, there were some soldiers at the Little Bighorn who were not only tenacious fighters, but also courageous. During the night of June 25, fifteen soldiers from the Reno-Benteen contingent risked their lives by going down to the river for water for their wounded comrades. They had to work their way through brush and rough terrain, and the Lakota and Northern Cheyenne who were waiting in the dark. The members of the water detail fought their way to the river and back. Rightly, they were decorated for their bravery.

It should be noted, however, that the three engagements over two days at the Little Bighorn were probably the first time that the Seventh Cavalry fought a native military force on an equal basis. At the Washita (in Kansas) in 1868, Custer's attacking force was eight hundred men strong against Black Kettle's village of three hundred—not all of them warriors. Although Custer was able to divide his forces for a potent four-pronged attack and take control of the village in only a few minutes, he still had a fight on his hands. Sporadic firing from Cheyenne men and boys hidden in the trees, and from along the Washita River, and from the nearby hills was an unexpected challenge. And after sundown, Cheyenne warriors returned, perhaps as many as a thousand or more, and surrounded what remained of the village. Custer, realizing he was outnumbered, withdrew his men. At the Little Bighorn, however, he did not have the option to withdraw from the field. He had no choice but to fight the kind of cavalry engagement in which the Lakota and Cheyenne excelled.

Three hundred soldiers of the Seventh Cavalry found their final resting place at the Little Bighorn. The spin doctors of the day wrote sensational news accounts and fueled the fires of revenge because the "elite" Seventh Cavalry had been "massacred" by savages. But the truth is, pound for pound, man for man, the soldiers who rode into the valley of the Little Bighorn were not equal to the Lakota and Northern Cheyenne as fighters. They did not have the years of training and individual skills at combat arms.

Furthermore, their duty was determined by the generals and policy makers who sent them on the mission to capture and kill Indians. Their fate was sealed when their commander divided his tired, exhausted force into four columns, and because Custer believed that the Lakota would break and run at the sight of soldiers.

In spite of being outnumbered, the Seventh Cavalry had considerable firepower. Perhaps they actually believed that righteousness was on their side as well, and thereby expected to be victorious. Many of them were probably surprised, therefore, at the level of ferocity and skill with which the Lakota and Northern Cheyenne warriors fought.

No doubt the soldiers tried to perform the duty they were sent out to do. But they failed. Ironically, their failure was commemorated and a monument was raised to them. The real irony is that the Long Knives did not die defending their nation against invaders. They were the invaders.

TEN

Weaponry

Bows and arrows

AROUND 1840, the Lakota had fairly consistent access to iron in the form of metal pots, the flat hoops from wooden barrels, and wagon wheel rims. Some of that material was acquired in trade or after white people had discarded it. Iron was used by the Lakota to make knives, lance points, and arrowheads for hunting and warfare. The iron was either melted down or cut with a cold chisel or, if available, a hacksaw. The consistent availability of iron was a benefit to the Lakota because they could make knives and projectile points with it faster than ones from stone. (After about 1850, the skill to make stone projectile points began to be a lost art.) But of all the weapons in the Lakota hunter/warrior's arsenal improved by iron, none were more so than the bow and arrow. Until they were mostly supplanted by firearms, the bow and arrow had been the premiere weapons for hunting and warfare. In fact, expert marksmanship with the bow and arrow was a prerequisite for being a Lakota fighting man and hunter. Boys were given bows around the age of five, and by the early teens, and sometimes sooner, many could frequently hit grasshoppers on the fly.

No one knows when the bow was acquired or invented, but it has been in North America for thousands of years. The arrow is older, strange as that may seem, and it was originally part of the weapon known as the atlatl, or spear thrower.

The atlatl consisted of two main parts: the handle and the projectile, called the dart. The top, or end, of the handle fit the back end of the dart. Its length and weight were used to throw the dart, propelling it for distances of a hundred yards or more. The dart was essentially a long, slender arrow shaft—about four feet or more—and fletched on the back end to give it stability in flight. So when the bow came along, the design of the dart was retained, but the shaft was shortened to about two feet, and became the arrow. (The exact arrow length varied from culture to culture and tribe to tribe, depending on factors such as specific use, materials, and size of the bow.)

Old stories among the Lakota say the moon gave them the bow, and one has only to look at the thinnest sliver of the new waxing moon to understand why. That configuration is the design for the Lakota bow: thickest in the middle, front to back and side to side, and tapered to the end of each limb, or wing. Paired with the arrow, it was the preferred weapon of hunters and warriors for generations.

On the northern plains of North America, the bow and arrow served the Lakota well. Hunters were able to bring down buffalo, bear, elk, deer, and antelope as well as smaller game. Survival depended on this type of skill and ability because food and raw materials required for day-to-day survival were procured by the hunter. How much he procured, or if he was able to do so at all, was determined in large part by his marksmanship. And hitting the target was no easy feat. The most vulnerable area on most large animals is only about eighteen inches in diameter. And the hunter could be as far away as fifty yards. If he missed that target, his family would not have food and the raw materials for clothing. The fact that the Lakota thrived on the northern plains under these circumstances—and particularly before the acquisition of firearms—is testament to the astounding skill of the hunter.

In one remarkable example, an army officer stationed at Fort Laramie in the 1850s wrote of an experience with two young Lakota boys. He described how he planted his pencil upright at the top of an anthill and invited the two youths to shoot at it with bows and arrows. He was astonished when one of them broke the pencil in half from a distance of slightly more than ten paces. The officer clearly did not realize that the bow was the premiere weapon for the Lakota, and that the boys had been trained to use it since about the age of four. The boy who broke that pencil was well on his way to reaching a high level of skill, and he may well have been at the Little Bighorn some twenty years later. At that point in his life, shooting a bow was second nature. Most Lakota archers, by their early teens, could launch ten to fifteen arrows in the space of a minute. That rate of firing only increased with age. Therefore, in the hands of a skilled archer, the bow was deadly.

Whether with gun or bow, experienced shooters know that in order to become proficient it is necessary to master the basic techniques of aiming. A rifle and bow are different, and the techniques of shooting them are different, but the act of aiming requires the same steadiness. The shooter also needs a good eye to judge distance and good concentration to focus on the target. Some shooters have an innate ability, while others have to develop their skill with years of practice.

Even though more and more Lakota acquired firearms of

some kind, the bow and arrow never became obsolete. At the very least, they were carried as backup. And many men preferred them for hunting because they were virtually silent. Furthermore, powder, lead balls, percussion caps, and bullets were often difficult to obtain, but the raw materials to manufacture bows and arrows were easily available. Because arrows were handcrafted—a time-consuming process—they were very valuable. Arrowheads especially were, in fact, regularly recovered from the battlefield.

Some of Major Reno's men experienced firsthand the effectiveness of the bow and arrow. After Reno's initial attack stalled and he was routed and chased into a grove of trees near the river, the bow and arrow—albeit briefly—came into play. Lakota archers shot arrows into the trees from behind cover, using a rainbow trajectory so that they could shoot from cover. Several of them lifted arrows high and let them fall into the trees among the soldiers and their horses. An arrow hissing down from the sky from an unseen shooter can be very unnerving, especially if it finds a target. This added to the chaos and confusion.

The generation of warriors who fought at the Little Bighorn was likely the last to use the bow and arrow in combat on a large scale. Many continued to make them to use for hunting, especially after being forced onto reservations. Because firearms were initially confiscated, making bows and arrows was also a way to quietly defy white authority. A few enterprising old men made them to sell to curious whites. Fortunately, when that last generation of traditional warriors passed on in the 1920s and 1930s, the bow and arrow did not die completely with them. A few, here and there, taught their sons the skills to handcraft them. So that knowledge has somehow survived. Though not many Lakota today know the true and ancient heritage of the bow and arrow, it does still live on in a few.

Guns and bullets

FIREARMS FIRST CAME into the lives of the Lakota when they were still in the lake country of what is now Minnesota, prior to 1700. The Anishinabe or Ojibway people traded for firearms from the French and drove the Lakota out of the region. After they settled on the northern plains, they consistently began to see firearms in the hands of the white trappers and traders, mostly French, who traveled up and down the Missouri River. It was not until about 1840 onward that the Lakota began acquiring firearms little by little, mostly by trade. While every Lakota adult male wanted a rifle, especially for warfare, acquiring it was never easy. Aside from trading, stealing or capturing one in battle was practically the only means for a man to get his hands on a firearm. By 1876, it is likely than more than half of all Lakota males had at least one firearm of some kind, and a few were lucky to have more than one.

Many oral accounts from the Lakota and Northern Cheyenne participants and observers describe the continuous gunfire during the second engagement of the Battle of the Little Bighorn. "Like someone tearing a cloth," one man said. That sound indicates the intensity of the battle and speaks to the fact that a significant number of Lakota and Northern Cheyenne fighting men had firearms.

Of continued special interest to historians is the number of repeating rifles, especially Winchesters, used against the Seventh Cavalry. That number, based on records kept by officials of the

Indian Bureau, is mostly conjecture and dubious at best. Due to altering here and there to appease the anger of those in the army and the government searching for a more logical reason behind the decisive defeat of the Seventh, the Indian Bureau's figures are skewed. Some advantage in firepower, taking into consideration all of the various kinds of firearms used by warriors, may have been possible simply because of the numerical superiority in this case. But how many repeating rifles would have tipped the balance to an *overwhelming* advantage cannot be known. Without a doubt, the Lakota and Northern Cheyenne did have repeating rifles, but a rifle in hand did not always mean an adequate supply of ammunition. Gall had two basic reasons for having several of his warriors dismount and take deliberate aim: one, to take better advantage of marksmanship skills, and two, to conserve ammunition by making every shot count. The greatest advantage of a repeating rifle is the rate of fire, or shot after shot without having to pause to reload. That advantage is useful as long as there is sufficient ammunition.

While the oral accounts of continuous gunfire in the second engagement seem to suggest significant use of repeating rifles, there are other factors that should be considered. Because of the shortage of ammunition, many warriors held their fire until they were at close range, thereby increasing the odds for a hit. This tactic was employed by warriors with pistols; percussion muzzle-loading rifles; or the various kinds of single-shot, heavy-caliber rifles.

We will likely never know the exact number of repeating rifles used by the warriors, or the extent of their ammunition supply for all their firearms. But we do know that ammunition was always in short supply for hunting and warfare.

On the other side of the issue, there are two indisputable facts: One, every soldier carried, or had available to him, one rifle and one pistol. The rifle was the Springfield carbine, a .45–55-caliber, breech-loading single shot. Its effective range was five hundred yards. The pistol was a .45-caliber, single-action, six-shot revolver. Two, every soldier had available to him a hundred rounds for his rifle and twenty-five for his pistol. Furthermore, if a soldier lost or expended all his ammunition, he could borrow or scrounge from a fellow soldier, because all the standard-issue rifles were the same. The same was true for pistols.

History tends to focus more on the second engagement in the overall Battle of the Little Bighorn—the annihilation of Lieutenant Colonel George A. Custer and his five companies—as *the* battle, or at least the most important of the three engagements. Yet reports on the Reno-Benteen action over the course of two days show that just over thirty-eight thousand rounds of rifle ammunition and a bit over twenty-nine hundred pistol rounds were expended. Some were probably lost in the chaos and confusion.

That number of bullets—nearly forty-one thousand—was possibly more than the Lakota and Northern Cheyenne expended in all three engagements over the two days. There is, of course, no definitive accounting of the number of rounds expended by Custer's five companies before they were all killed. Historians contend that the Seventh was defeated because they were outnumbered and outgunned. There is no disputing that there were more warriors than soldiers. But if the assumption that the soldiers were outgunned means that the victors were better armed overall *and* had more bullets, that assumption is difficult to substantiate.

Perhaps a more compelling issue than the number of rounds expended, on both sides, was the effect the bullets had. American field commanders in Vietnam were able to ascertain that for every enemy killed, *fifty thousand* small arms rounds were expended—meaning bullets from rifles, handguns, and light machine guns. Extrapolating the same kind of statistic from the Battle of the Little Bighorn may not result in a definitive rounds-to-kill ratio for the victors or the losers. However, the fact is that far more soldiers than warriors were killed.

The age range of the Lakota and Northern Cheyenne fighting men is unknown, but a safe estimate would be between thirty to forty years old. Men in that age range would have been in the physical prime of their lives and likely the best group as marksmen. They also would have fought with a firearm of some type and delivered the best rounds-to-kill ratio of fire.

Effectively covering a field of fire, either as an individual or a unit, is to deliver rounds *accurately* into a particular position or area, that is, hitting the target. Effectiveness of fire, more so than the number of rounds expended, has to be regarded as a primary factor in the outcome of the battle. Furthermore, except for Reno's attempted entrenchment in the trees along the river, and later the Reno-Benteen barricaded position, most of the engagements did not involve static or entrenched positions. This meant that both sides had to shoot mostly at moving targets. Therefore, although historians have a tendency to downplay the marksmanship of the warriors, they seem to have been far more skilled at hitting moving targets, especially in the second engagement.

There is yet another factor frequently mentioned within the broad story of the Little Bighorn, but it is perhaps not accorded enough credibility. A number of the Springfield carbines jammed on the soldiers during the fighting. Anecdotal evidence alludes to copper-cased cartridges cracking and fusing to the walls of the rifles' chambers, forcing soldiers to extract the spent cartridges with a tool of some kind. Then any metal bits or shavings, or the casing's rim that had separated, had to be cleaned out before the next round could be loaded. This would, of course, reduce the soldiers' rate of fire considerably.

The skill, training, experience, and tactics employed by fighting men and women of any army are some of the factors that determine the outcome of a battle. Weapons are just as important as weather and terrain. In spite of the tremendous firepower taken into battle by the U.S. Seventh Cavalry on June 25 and 26, 1876, they were defeated. How they were defeated will continue to be a topic of debate, and the weapons used by both sides in the Battle of the Little Bighorn will be part of it. There were other weapons not carried in the hand, however, that were just as effective, if not more so, than the bows and arrows and the guns and bullets. And yet those weapons are rarely mentioned. Those weapons can and do enhance the ones carried in the hand, and they can effectively neutralize superior numbers or superior firepower. At the Battle of the Little Bighorn, the devotion and commitment of the Lakota and Northern Cheyenne warriors were the most powerful weapons of all.

ELEVEN

They Took the Fat

Mixed messages, belligerence, and disease

NO ONE KNOWS EXACTLY when the Lakota first had contact with white people. Very possibly it was as early as the late 1600s. Then, in the lakes region of Minnesota, their enemies the Anishinabe had a trading relationship with the French. So the Lakota would have at least known that white people existed.

The first European documented contact was with a party of French explorers who traveled up the Missouri River in the early 1720s. Atop a bluff overlooking the confluence of the Bad and Missouri rivers, they buried an engraved lead tablet to mark their travels—a "Kilroy was here" sort of gesture. By most Lakota accounts, they were heavily armed and belligerent. It is not beyond reason to suggest that their belligerence was their undoing, since the Blackfeet killed them all.

For nearly eighty years after that, the Lakota seemed to have been spared consistent contact. A few traders did take the risk to travel into the upper Missouri River region now and then. But that changed in the summer of 1804, when up the Missouri against the current came a large wooden boat with a square sail, the first of many strange sights associated with white people. Accompanying it were two wooden canoes. It was the largest group of white men the Sicangu Lakota had ever seen. One of the men had black skin, and with the group was a large black dog. In the annals of Euro-American history, this was, of course, the Lewis and Clark expedition.

The white men camped on an island in the river south of the mouth of the Bad River and stayed a few days. They offered gifts and did strange ceremonies while dressed in their finest. There was no clear communication because the Sicangu could not understand the whites' spoken language, or the hand sign that one of them used. And no one among the whites could understand or speak Lakota.

The encounter could have turned out badly, but cooler heads prevailed. At one point, after the Sicangu were allowed to inspect the largest boat, a misunderstanding precipitated a tense standoff. The whites cocked their rifles and pointed them at the warriors lined up on the shore. One of the older more experienced warriors persuaded the others to move off, and bloodshed was averted. On the other hand, a few stories handed down among the Lakota suggest that Lewis and Clark may have taken up to four Lakota as hostages, to ensure safe passage northward up the river. Whatever the details, it is interesting to note that of this encounter, Captain William Clark wrote sometime later in his journal:

> These are the vilest miscreants of the savage race, and must ever remain the pirates of the Missouri, until such measures are pursued, by our government, as will make them feel a dependence on its will for their supply of merchandise.

That dependence threatened by Clark was finally manifested seventy years later when white hunters killed nearly all of the buffalo on the northern plains.

But if, during their sojourn among the Sicangu Lakota, Lewis and Clark had been able to communicate accurately the message they carried with them from President Jefferson, their expedition might well have ended at the Bad River confluence. That message was that the United States now owned the land, and the tribes had a Great Father in Washington, and this new Great Father wanted his "red children" to make peace with their neighbors and trade only with Americans.

After a good laugh, the warrior leaders might well have turned their men loose against the explorers.

The expedition went farther north and then west. As we now know, owing to the fact that they were saved from starvation and given horses and directions by several tribes, they successfully completed their mission. Because of that success, other whites followed.

Boats much larger than the Lewis and Clark keelboat became a familiar sight up and down the Missouri in the years that followed. Steamboats brought people and trade goods. In the late 1830s, one such vessel brought something more. On its northwest journey it stopped off at Whetstone Landing, near the present town of Pickstown, South Dakota, and off-loaded supplies and a few passengers, and a deadly disease as well. It proceeded north to Mandan and Hidatsa territory.

Smallpox came with the supplies, or perhaps the people. During that summer, nearly a thousand Lakota died as the disease spread like a prairie fire. Trying to run from the disease, the people abandoned their villages, burning some with dead bodies still inside the dwellings. For years afterward, many village sites stood abandoned, marked by only skeletal lodge poles until they finally fell.

Later the Lakota learned that the people who lived in earth lodges along the upper Missouri also suffered greatly from the same scourge. Less than one hundred of two thousand Mandan survived, and their allies, the Hidatsa, were ravaged as well. There was no weapon carried by the whites that was ever feared as much as the diseases they brought with them.

Rolling wood

IN THE EARLY 1840s, first the Sicangu and then the Oglala noticed a consistent movement of white people through the southern fringes of their territory. In what is now northwestern Nebraska, the Sicangu saw long lines of wagons pulled by mules and oxen. They were heading west, following the Shell, or North Platte, River corridor. That corridor cut across what is now southeastern Wyoming, through Oglala territory. Eventually, the wagons turned south past Elk Mountain (overlooking present-day Casper, Wyoming) and moved farther west into Shoshoni country.

As was the case with every new idea or object brought by the whites, the Lakota had to find a name or description. The wagon was *can pagmiyanpi* (chan bah-gmee-yahn-be), or "wood that is rolled."

Curiosity drew daring young men for a closer look. Although the first face-to-face encounters were often uneasy, there were no outright conflicts. Often there was trade of some kind. The young men reported seeing women and children in the wagons, which were loaded with what had to be possessions. Herds of cattle were driven along for fresh meat. With the cold autumn winds, the wagons stopped coming, so the Lakota shrugged and went on with their lives. The following summer, however, behind plodding oxen and two, sometimes three, teams of mules, more wagons came creaking and clunking along from east to west.

Knowing that whites carried terrible diseases, the elders advised little or no contact, not knowing what else to do, since the whites appeared to be merely passing through. Summer after summer they came. For one or two summers some of the whites, obviously without mules or oxen, pushed or pulled two-wheeled carts piled high with their things. But strangely, they traveled on the other side of the river, and overall, there were more and more wagons. Every new line followed the trail left by the previous train until the ruts of their road cut deep into the earth. Except for the basic concern that the white travelers were trespassing on Lakota territory, there was no significant reason for alarm. After the first few years, however, the Lakota saw the land along the trail spoiled by dead animals and discarded possessions, and the graves of the emigrants who had died along the route. Furthermore, buffalo herds that migrated across or along the Shell River altered their usual trails. Then one summer someone in one of the wagons fired on Lakota boys riding in close to have a look, and killed one.

The immediate response was not retaliatory, though some younger warriors wanted to attack in revenge. Groups of warriors stopped the trains and began demanding payment to travel through their territory. That angered the travelers and laid the foundation for conflict.

For about twenty years the Oregon Trail, as it was primarily known to the white emigrants who used it, was the main avenue of migration for whites from east to west. The Lakota did not know that the reason so many whites were migrating was due to hard economic times in their country. Their concern was the effect on their lives and territory. Also unknown to them, the emigrants had demanded help from their government for protection from the people on whose lands they were trespassing.

Peace talkers

A FUR-TRADING COMPANY had established a post in Oglala Lakota territory along the Shell River called Fort John (in what is now southeastern Wyoming). In response to emigrant fears, the U.S. Army purchased the trading post and turned it into a military outpost, and renamed it Fort Laramie. It was to that outpost that many tribes of the northern plains were called for a treaty meeting in the summer of 1851.

Not surprisingly, many tribes responded. From the north came the Blackfeet and the Crow. The Shoshoni came from the west. Out of the northeast came the Mandan, Hitatsa, and Arikara. From the south came the Arapaho, and, of course, there were the Cheyenne. Since it was their territory, many Lakota were there along with the Dakota and Nakota from the east.

Though the Blackfeet, the Crow, and the Shoshoni were deep in enemy country, there were no clashes. For nearly a month ancient enemies and allies lived in peace, bound by their curiosity about the whites. In between horse racing, dancing, and trading, the leaders of the various tribes assembled to listen to the *wolakotiye woglakapi*, or the "peace talkers," of the whites, as the Lakota understood them to be. Fortunately, they were led by Thomas Fitzpatrick, once a mountain man and known to many different tribes. Some called him Broken Hand.

But the presence of Broken Hand notwithstanding, the peace commissioners failed to deliver their message clearly, owing to the shortage of skilled translators who could speak nine different languages, not to mention a variety of subdialects. The various tribes more or less explained the goings-on to one another and managed to get the gist of all the haranguing.

The government, as it turned out, wanted agreement on three points. First, the various tribes were to stop fighting one another and live in peace thereafter. Second, the white emigrants using the Oregon Trail were not to be molested, under penalty of punishment by the Great Father, who could see if the Indians were bad. About this latter statement, an old Lakota was said to have suggested that the trail must be "holy" in some fashion. He was, of course, being facetious, but thereafter the Oregon Trail became the "Holy" Road to the Lakota. Third, territorial boundaries were established, primarily for the Lakota, Dakota, and Nakota. In payment for their agreement to those conditions, the gathered tribes would be paid annuities in the form of goods.

Anyone reading history written by white historians is led to believe that the native tribes who came to Fort Laramie in 1851 accepted the authority of the United States. The peace commissioners at that time presumed to have authority over a region they presumed to own, and over the people who lived within it. Most of the native leaders at Fort Laramie questioned the overall purpose of the gathering and did not like the paternalistic attitude of the whites. And only a few of them felt the whites had any credibility.

Because native leaders "signed" the documents, the United States took that as full understanding and agreement to the treaty, and recognition by those native tribes that the United States had authority over them. Native leaders signed the documents—actually they made X's while an interpreter wrote their names—because they were invited to do so and because they understood that gifts for the people were in the offing. As far as those people and their leaders were concerned, their territory was their territory, and many of them scoffed at the idea that whites were in control. As a case in point, old hostilities with ancient enemies were resumed in direct violation of one of the conditions the peace commissioners thought that the native leaders had understood and agreed to.

Whatever the native people and their leaders thought, the whites would not go away. For the Lakota, the uneasiness and anxiety over the Holy Road was a consequence of conflicts instigated by the white emigrants. Yet the mind-set of the United States and its peace commissioners was that the trouble had been instigated by the Lakota, and certainly would be again. Furthermore, the United States was prepared to punish offenders, tacitly assuming no trouble would be instigated by the emigrants.

Interestingly, however, white-Lakota conflicts did not escalate on the Holy Road itself, but certainly because of it. White ethnocentrism was the catalyst.

The arrogance of the interloper

AN INCIDENT THAT OCCURRED in mid-August of 1854 was the beginning of what white historians refer to as the "Indian wars." Such a characterization implies that Indians started the war, and obscures the fact that whites were the invaders. The incident in question is an unwavering blueprint for the attitude and actions of Euro-Americans, civilian or military, during those so-called Indian wars. And misunderstanding was at its core.

A cow wandered into a Sicangu Lakota camp and became a nuisance. A visiting Mniconju Lakota killed it and distributed the meat to elderly people. The cow's owner, a Mormon, complained to the commander at Fort Laramie. Conquering Bear, a self-appointed spokesman, went to the fort and offered more than adequate compensation for the cow. The offer was refused, and the owner stubbornly wanted the cow's killer to be punished. A newly posted West Point graduate, Lieutenant John Grattan, obtained permission to apprehend the thief. He arrived at the Sicangu encampment with thirty soldiers and two mountain howitzers, and a drunken half-breed interpreter. Grattan demanded the surrender of the Mniconju Lakota who killed the cow. The offer of compensation was repeated, but the drunken interpreter botched the translation—on purpose, some Lakota felt. Grattan was incensed and ordered his soldiers to open fire with rifles and howitzers. One of the first casualties was Conquering Bear. Sicangu and Oglala fighting men, who had gathered in the camp, responded in anger. They opened fire and chased down and killed the soldiers, including Grattan and the interpreter. It is, of course, known to white history as the Grattan Massacre.

A teenage Lakota boy was one of the witnesses to the incident. At the time, he still had his boyhood name of Jiji, or Light Hair. A few years later he became Crazy Horse.

Almost exactly a year later, the U.S. Army avenged Grattan. Near the Blue Water River in southern Sicangu territory (now northwestern Nebraska), a village under the leadership of Little

Thunder, Spotted Tail, and Iron Shell was attacked by troops from Fort Kearny (in Nebraska Territory) under General William Harney.

Harney parleyed with the leaders, demanding the "murderers" of Lieutenant Grattan and his soldiers be turned over to him. The fact that Grattan instigated his own demise was obviously not important to the general. While he had Little Thunder and the other leaders as a captive audience away from the village, most of his troops sneaked up on the village and attacked. Though they were outnumbered and outgunned, the Lakota accounted well for themselves. In spite of the heroic actions of Spotted Tail and Iron Shell—the former managed to kill ten soldiers with a captured sword before he was seriously wounded—eighty people were killed and about seventy taken prisoner, mostly women and children.

At dusk, well after the attack, a group of boys and young men returned from hunting and saw smoke rising from the encampment. One of them rode into what was left of the village, finding scattered objects, burning lodges, and dead bodies. He briefly followed a long column he saw in the distance: the soldiers with their captives. But he turned aside to aid a young Cheyenne woman whose husband and child had been killed. He took her to safety in the direction the survivors had fled, into the sand hills (of central Nebraska). Once again, that boy's name was Jiji, or Light Hair.

In the days and weeks that followed, Harney swept northward through Lakota territory, untouched. News of his attack on Little Thunder's peaceful village was reported in the eastern newspapers, and the general was vilified and dubbed Squaw Killer.

Among the Lakota, he was known as Winyan Wicakte, or Woman Killer.

Gold changes things

THE OREGON TRAIL was still busy every summer. In its twenty years, some 350,000 emigrants used it, and essentially laid waste to the land. To this day, ruts still remain as mute testimony to one of the most intrusive migrations in North American history.

The next major intrusion was the Bozeman Trail in the early 1860s. A man named John Bozeman marked a trail from what is now south central Wyoming along the foothills of the Big Horn Mountains northward. This was the southwestern edge of Oglala Lakota territory. The trail eventually went beyond the Yellowstone River and west to what is now central Montana, ending at the gold fields near the present town of Virginia City. Bozeman marked the trail by pounding wooden stakes into the ground.

The trail brought gold seekers. But an unwanted diversion occurred in Arapaho territory to the south, in what is now eastern Colorado. A Cheyenne and Arapaho camp along Sand Creek was attacked in late November of 1864 by Colorado militia. In command was Colonel John Chivington, a Methodist minister. The seven hundred soldiers killed over two hundred people, in spite of the fact that the Cheyenne and Arapaho leaders flew both a flag of truce and an American flag, having been told to do so to invoke government protection. Many of the dead were horribly mutilated by the militia, who wore body parts on their uniforms as they paraded victoriously through Denver.

The Cheyenne and Arapaho called for revenge, and Lakota warriors responded. Crazy Horse, of the Oglala, and his renowned uncle Spotted Tail, of the Sicangu, were among them. Though they successfully attacked the settlement at Julesburg in the Moon of Popping Trees, January, as well as many outlying ranches, the campaign slowed because whites in the region avoided contact with the formidable forces put into the field by the Cheyenne, Arapaho, and Lakota. Still enraged, the combined force moved north at the invitation of the Lakota, and a large gathering of the three nations wintered in the Powder River country (what is now central and north central Wyoming).

The ensuing winter and spring solidified the Lakota/Cheyenne/Arapaho alliance. Warrior ceremonies were conducted and horses were strengthened on the fresh spring browse in anticipation of more warfare against the whites. Attempted incursions by three separate U.S. Army columns were effectively repulsed. Still seeking revenge, however, the Cheyenne pushed for an attack against an army post near the Platte River bridge, an emigrant crossing over the North Platte on the Oregon Trail. Plans were made, and a large force headed south in the middle of summer.

Overall, the fighting at and around the Platte River crossing was not a resounding success. A significant ambush was spoiled by overeager young warriors, and the Cheyenne lost a significant war leader, not to mention that the soldiers acquitted themselves well against a larger force. The only success, called the Battle of Red Buttes, was earned by the Cheyenne against a column of soldiers escorting a supply train.

After regrouping in the Powder River country, the three-nation gathering concluded. Most of the Cheyenne and Arapaho returned south to their own territory, and the Lakota turned their attention to the Bozeman Trail. In late summer a large column of soldiers entered the Powder River region after stopping off at Fort Laramie. Word was out quickly that the soldiers had been brought in to build forts. The Lakota were outraged because the new column had arrived before negotiations seeking permission to build the forts had been concluded.

The column was a regiment of the Eighteenth Infantry under the command of Colonel Henry Carrington; it comprised some seven hundred men, about a thousand head of cattle, and over two hundred wagons pulled by mules. They built two forts within a span of months. The first, Reno, was really only a refurbishment of one near a dry fork of the Powder River. The second, Philip Kearny, was built from the ground up farther north along the Bozeman Trail, halfway between the present towns of Buffalo and Sheridan, Wyoming. A third, C. F. Smith, was eventually built along the Bighorn to the north, near what is now Hardin, Montana.

The Lakota concentrated on the second of the outposts, Fort Philip Kearny. Days after the soldiers first arrived and bivouacked on Buffalo Creek (called Piney by the soldiers), and before the fort was built, the Lakota attacked and captured nearly two hundred horses and mules. Other attacks followed, though not many casualties were inflicted against the soldiers. After the fort was finished, the Lakota became especially frustrated because the soldiers could not be drawn out to fight. They carried out raids against the travelers on the Bozeman Trail, many of whom stopped off at the fort. When wood-cutting and haying details were sent out from the fort, the Lakota attacked them. That was generally the pattern of activity until that winter.

More soldiers arrived early in the winter of 1866. Notable among them was one Captain William Fetterman, who was openly disdainful about natives and their fighting ability. He was known to have boasted that with eighty good men he could ride through the Sioux (Lakota) nation.

Early in December, a patrol was attacked, but only two soldiers were killed. Two weeks later the Lakota nearly succeeded in an ambush, but young warriors attacked prematurely and the soldiers escaped. Two days later, however, they tried again.

The foolishness of one

ON THE BITTERLY COLD MORNING of December 21, 1866, the wood supply wagons emerged from the fort, heading for the pinery a few miles west of the fort. Within sight of the fort's lookouts the wagons were attacked. A rescue column led by Captain Fetterman was sent out, ironically numbering eighty men (including two civilians). Half of the column was mounted, and half was on foot. Out of nowhere, ten mounted warriors led by the twenty-five-year-old Crazy Horse attacked the rescue column. Incredibly, Fetterman abandoned his rescue mission and chased Crazy Horse. Unknown to Fetterman, Crazy Horse had been picked to lead decoys in yet another attempt to draw the soldiers out into a battle. Fetterman had swallowed the ruse.

Crazy Horse and his decoys led Fetterman across frozen, snow-covered ground, taunting the soldiers with a show of superb horsemanship, and exchanging gunfire with the pursuing soldiers. The chase proceeded northward for over four miles until it reached Lodge Trail Ridge. Fetterman halted briefly, but only because he had been ordered not to proceed beyond Lodge

Trail. But the taunting warriors drew him off the ridge and then led him even farther north, interestingly, along the Bozeman Trail itself. At the bottom of a long, gradual slope, Crazy Horse and his decoys—who, amazingly, had suffered no casualties—rode a crisscross pattern. At that signal, at least five hundred warriors (predominantly Lakota with some Northern Cheyenne and a few Northern Arapaho) rose from the banks and gullies on either side of the ridge and attacked.

The battle was joined, and though the soldiers fought fiercely as they attempted to retrace the trail back to the fort, all were killed in less than an hour. Historians call it the Fetterman Massacre. But Lakota, Cheyenne, and Arapaho participants said the soldiers fought well and exacted high casualties. Because a Cheyenne seer had foreseen a victory over one hundred soldiers, the Lakota called it the Battle of the Hundred in the Hand.

A consequence of the battle was Carrington's removal as the commander of Fort Philip Kearny.

New rifles and more peace talkers

THE SOLDIERS POSTED at the forts had the opportunity to avenge Fetterman, however. Several months later, a large force of Cheyenne attacked a civilian detail putting up hay near Fort C. F. Smith. They and their escort of twenty soldiers successfully defended themselves, owing largely to new rifles. Their old muzzle-loading, single-shot Springfield rifles had been replaced with breechloaders, which could be reloaded and fired much faster. The next day, nearly eighty miles to the south, that intense skirmish was replayed, with much the same results.

Thirty-two soldiers came under attack at a wood-cutting camp several miles west of Fort Philip Kearny. The soldiers took cover in a circle of detached wagon boxes and grimly defended themselves. The Lakota, expecting the customary pause in firing as soldiers reloaded muzzle-long rifles, were surprised when there was no break in the firing. Mounted and foot charges proved more harmful for the attackers. The first attack had begun in the morning, and the battle ended at noon. A detachment from the fort arrived with a howitzer, and the Lakota wisely withdrew.

Other factors, aside from guns and bullets, were at work far from the battles along the Bozeman Trail, factors that would bring an end to the conflict. A seven-member peace commission was appointed, which included General William Sherman and General William Harney. Harney, of course, was infamous to the Lakota after his sneak attack on Little Thunder's camp on the Blue Water in 1855. The commission traveled to the northern plains, and to their first meeting at North Platte, Nebraska. There they got an earful of complaints and the ultimatum that whites would have to get out of Lakota country. Sherman, of course, rejected that notion and advised the Lakota to select a suitable place for a reservation and learn how to farm. After that display of paternalistic attitude, only one Lakota leader showed up for the next meeting two months later. When the commission members opened their session at Fort Laramie, no representatives of the Lakota were present. General Harney considered that to be unforgivable insolence, and he wondered how many troops would be necessary to launch a punitive campaign against the Lakota.

The following spring, of 1868, the peace commissioners returned to Fort Laramie and offered a treaty. It was signed by representatives of the Sicangu, Oglala, and Mniconju Lakota, and by the Ihantunwan Nakota as well as the Arapaho. The treaty ended the conflict along the Bozeman Trail, also known as Red Cloud's War. Red Cloud was, at the time, a significant military leader among the Lakota. He had been chosen by the U.S. Army and the peace commissioners as their "treaty chief."

But the treaty had also put limits on the Lakota world. The Lakota had accepted a reservation that amounted to the entire western half of the present state of South Dakota. They were also given hunting rights in portions of what are now North Dakota, eastern Wyoming, and northern Nebraska. Those areas were referred to as "ceded territory." But, of course, the clause read ". . . so long as buffalo may range in sufficient numbers to justify the chase." A clause open to interpretation was one thing; actual numbers of buffalo still in Lakota territory would be another.

After the forts along the Bozeman Trail were abandoned, Red Cloud accepted the U.S. government's offer of his own agency and moved to Camp Robinson, in what is now northwestern Nebraska. Spotted Tail, the Sicangu Lakota headman, also took up residence on his own agency. In one fell swoop, the United States effectively managed to neutralize two of the most influential Lakota leaders of the nineteenth century by using the power of persuasion. The government promised to take care of them for the rest of their lives and let them run their agencies as they saw fit, within the government's rules, of course. Years later, the government built a house for each "chief," after they moved north to what are now the Pine Ridge and Rosebud reservations.

On the other side of the issue, both leaders decided that further resistance of any kind against the more numerous whites was futile. Both, after all, had traveled to Washington, D.C., and had seen firsthand the apparent power of the United States, embodied in the unimaginably large cities and a population resembling a field of anthills. Furthermore, they reasoned, some control over their own lives was better than none at all. As Red Cloud and Spotted Tail saw it, the Lakota nation had lost control over its own destiny. But by succumbing to life on the agency, each of them had aided that loss of control. Because they were influential men, thousands of people followed them to those agencies, including a significant number of warriors.

The iron road, a fortune in hides, and gold, again

IN REALITY, Red Cloud did not win the war for the Bozeman Trail. The United States saw an easier access to the gold fields of Montana. A railroad line along the Yellowstone River to the north seemed more logical and less contentious. But the apparent abandonment of the Bozeman Trail did not mean that whites had moved out of Lakota territory entirely. A few military outposts remained: Fort Laramie, of course, as well as the new posts of Fort Fetterman (near present-day Douglas, Wyoming) and Fort Caspar near the Platte River crossing (at present-day Casper, Wyoming). And as the Lakota learned early on, where there were soldiers, civilians followed and stayed. But there was a greater concern: The buffalo had dwindled noticeably in number.

In the spring of 1868, General Sherman wrote to his superior, General Philip Sheridan, and urged that the sportsmen of the United States and Great Britain be invited to come west to shoot buffalo. "Gentlemen" hunters, sportsmen all, did come west and hunted buffalo. Rifle muzzles pointing out of both sides of railroad passenger cars were not an unusual sight. Trains would slow at the sight of even a single animal within rifle range.

By the early 1870s, Lakota hunters had to travel far beyond usual buffalo migratory trails to find any. They had no way of knowing, of course, that buffalo hides had become extremely popular in New England for everything, including furniture upholstery, saddles, shoes, and harnesses. Individual hides fetched nearly four dollars each. Buffalo hides became a way for a man to pursue his fortune, so killing buffalo became piecework. A reasonably good marksman with a .50-caliber rifle could kill 50 or more in one day. There were fantastic claims of individual hunters bringing down 120 or more in one day. Of course, only the hides were taken, leaving the rest of the carcass to rot. But buffalo hides were not the only possibility for fortunes to be made.

Rumors of gold in the Black Hills had been circulating. Ten companies of the United States Seventh Cavalry, under the command of Lieutenant Colonel George Custer, were sent to the Black Hills from Fort Abraham Lincoln in early July of 1874. The expedition was relatively short in duration—only two months. Custer was effusive, though totally inaccurate, when he said that gold quartz could be seen on almost every hill and in the very roots of the grass. The Lakota dubbed the expedition's route into the Black Hills the Thieves Road.

Of course, prospectors poured in. With a halfhearted nod to the provisions of the 1868 Fort Laramie Treaty, the U.S. Army made weak attempts to close the Black Hills. By 1875, there were hundreds, if not thousands, of white prospectors in those mountains scratching, digging, and panning for gold. Unable to keep them out, the United States did the next best thing: It attempted to revise the Fort Laramie Treaty and buy the Black Hills outright.

When emotions ran high at the first meeting to discuss the sale, no agreement was reached. A tense standoff with guns pointed on both sides of the cultural aisle had shaken the treaty commissioners. Consequently, they left the region entirely. From a distance they opined that it was utterly necessary to teach the Lakota a lesson. The basis for that threat was, in their perspective, that the Lakota had made no attempts to abide by the 1868 treaty.

Strangely, however, sometime later the U.S. government waived an "agreement" they purported to have reached with certain Lakota leaders. They failed to disclose that they had threatened a few old men, past their prime as influential leaders, and coerced them to sign a document that agreed to the redrawing of the western boundary of the Great Sioux Reservation. The new boundary line was moved east of the Black Hills.

The United States was obviously not going to force white prospectors out of the Black Hills and leave the land and the gold to the Lakota. Gold was obviously of no use to the Lakota, so it was logical to take the land, one way or another. The peace commissioners and politicians failed to realize that, for the Lakota, it was not an issue of proprietorship of a resource. The issue was control of their territory and their lives. Of course, by 1875 most of the Lakota were already living on agencies on the dole of the United States, and therefore, the Euro-American perception was that the Lakota did not need the Black Hills.

An ultimatum and a message

NO TWO PEOPLE at the time were more painfully aware that most Lakota were living on agencies under the control of the whites than Sitting Bull and Crazy Horse. They and their people were still living the nomadic hunting life, though they had to contend with few resources and persistent white encroachment.

Two different messages were sent, almost concurrently, from two different leaders within months of each other. But the response to each would bring their causes together in such a way as to bring tragic results, immediately for one side and eventually for the other.

Late in 1875, President Ulysses Grant issued an ultimatum aimed at all native tribes in the West, but specifically intended for the Lakota. All free-roaming tribes were to report to a reservation by January 31, 1876, or risk being considered "hostile," and subject to apprehension by government troops. Early in 1876, Sitting Bull issued a call for the Lakota to gather in order to consider solutions to the continuing encroachment of white people. If Sitting Bull was aware of the U.S. government's ultimatum, it was not obvious. Grant certainly did not know about Sitting Bull's message.

At the same time Grant's ultimatum was dispatched, or perhaps before, the top generals in the U.S. Army were working on plans for a summer campaign against the Lakota. Knowing where both Sitting Bull and Crazy Horse were, they decided that a three-way pincer movement aimed for the Powder River–Yellowstone region would chase the Lakota into a trap. Sitting Bull, meanwhile, wanted the people to meet near Chalk Buttes, in what is now southeastern Montana. After a few hundred people arrived there in late April and early May, they began to migrate westward into the area the army had picked as the center of its trap.

Thousands of people were on the move because of those two messages. In one case, the weight of authority caused men in blue uniforms to pursue the duty they were given. How they might have felt individually about its purpose or worthiness was secondary to following orders. On the other hand, entire families responded to the weight of the message, or the reputation of the man who had sent it, or perhaps both. They saw their involvement as purposeful and exceedingly worthy of their individual commitment and participation for the good of the whole.

Trails, a trial, and errors

BEFORE THE FIRST GROUPS of Lakota met Sitting Bull at Chalk Buttes, one part of the trap intended to ensnare him had already been on the move. Brigadier General George Crook left Fort Fetterman on or about March 1 with twelve companies: two infantry and ten cavalry. They were more or less on a scouting expedition.

Crook proceeded north along the old Bozeman Trail. After waiting out a blizzard, he continued to the Tongue River, which was within a few days' march of the Yellowstone River. When no Indians were found, the column turned east toward the Powder River. Three companies of cavalry under Colonel J. J. Reynolds found horse tracks and followed them to an encampment along the Powder. Reynolds attacked at daybreak, assuming the camp was Lakota. In reality, it was Two Moons' Cheyenne on their way to the agency. With them were a few Lakota families led by He Dog, Crazy Horse's closest friend.

Though the initial attack was successful, the Cheyenne and Lakota fighters retaliated and recovered many of the horses the cavalry had taken. They gained the high ground and managed to pin Reynolds down, forcing him to retreat. Unrelenting, the

Cheyenne and Lakota pursued Reynolds for nearly a day before turning back.

Because of Reynolds's attack, both Two Moons and He Dog changed their minds about going on to the agency, resolving instead to join Crazy Horse. Crook subsequently brought charges against Reynolds, primarily because two dead soldiers were left in the field, and perhaps a wounded man as well. Though Colonel Reynolds defended himself vigorously, he and two of his company commanders were found guilty. Reynolds was suspended for a year.

At about the time Sitting Bull and the few Lakota bands with him initially arrived at Ash Creek, a few miles southeast of the Little Bighorn River, the second part of the trap—the eastern column—departed from Fort Abraham Lincoln on May 17. In command was Major General Alfred Terry. With him, of course, was the Seventh Cavalry, commanded by Lieutenant Colonel George Custer. The western column under Colonel John Gibbon had departed from Fort Ellis (near the present town of Bozeman, Montana) with 450 men.

When the eastern column reached the Powder River, about June 12, the second in command of the Seventh, Major Marcus Reno, was sent on a scouting expedition that took eight days. He went farther south along the Powder, turned west and crossed a tributary of the Powder and another of the Tongue, and then the Tongue River itself. On June 17, he arrived at Rosebud Creek. From there he turned north to the Yellowstone River, unaware that less than fifty miles to the south, the southern column under General George Crook was having its objective redirected by a determined force led by Crazy Horse.

After the debacle of the Reynolds court-martial, Crook

departed once again from Fort Fetterman, in May. His command consisted of ten companies of cavalry, five infantry, and civilian auxiliaries—a formidable force of just over 1,000 men. Shortly before June 17, 180 Crow and 90 Shoshoni scouts arrived to join Crook.

As Crook entered the Powder River country again, Lakota scouts kept a close watch on his column. As he continued north, two scouts were sent back to the Lakota encampment on Ash Creek, fifty miles to the north.

Crooks' scouts informed him that the Lakota were more than likely somewhere up along Rosebud Creek. The general ordered all haste to be made, even leaving supply wagons behind and putting his infantry on the backs of mules. On the night of the sixteenth of June, his nearly thirteen-hundred-man column made camp in a wide meadow in the valley of the Rosebud. Sometime after daybreak the next morning, as the column was eating and preparing to move again, gunfire erupted.

Unknown to Crook, of course, Crazy Horse had led a force of at least five hundred men—mostly Lakota with some Northern Cheyenne—through the night, a distance of fifty miles, and found Crook's camp.

Though Crook's soldiers responded immediately, Crazy Horse's attack was so swift and intense that company commanders could not communicate with Crook, and confusion ensued. It was a hard-fought battle, by all accounts. The soldiers fought well, but the mounted Lakota and Northern Cheyenne were in their element, and they kept continuous pressure on the pockets of soldiers forced to take up defensive positions. As the sun moved inexorably across the summer sky, the flow of battle favored first one side, and then the other. In truth, there were many different battles, each with its own movement and changing circumstance. Sometime in the afternoon, the Lakota infiltrated the Crow and Shoshoni scouts. The soldiers could only watch as the classic version of Plains Indians close combat was played out before them.

Later in the afternoon, Crazy Horse ordered a withdrawal, not because he was losing but because men and horses were exhausted and ammunition was running low. Strangely, as the Lakota and Northern Cheyenne began to leave the field, the soldiers made no significant or organized attempts to engage them further. Several companies of cavalry, dispatched by Crook earlier on some errant mission, happened to return as the Lakota moved away. A brief clash occurred before the soldiers returned to the main body, by now already starting to lick its wounds.

Crook buried his dead in the dark that night. In the days that followed, he turned his column back to the south, almost constantly harassed, guerrilla style, by a small force of Lakota and Northern Cheyenne. His withdrawal contributed significantly to the failure of the army's plan to capture the Lakota.

Long Knives on the Greasy Grass

AFTER SEVERAL WEEKS, the Gibbon and Terry columns met on the Yellowstone River as planned, at the mouth of the Powder River. There they were resupplied by steamboat. The two columns proceeded west to the mouth of the Tongue River. On the twenty-first of June, General Terry sent the Gibbon column (without Gibbon) up the Yellowstone to the Little Bighorn River. Terry was convinced that the Lakota were in the area south of the Yellowstone. The next day Terry sent Custer and the Seventh Cavalry to the mouth of the Rosebud with orders to follow it upstream until they found the Indian trail discovered by Reno's earlier scouting. From there Custer was to proceed farther upstream until he could enter the Little Bighorn valley directly from the south.

General Terry also ordered Custer to dispatch any information from his scouting to Colonel Gibbon, who would be waiting at the mouth of the Little Bighorn River. No such information ever came because no such scouting was ever carried out. Custer marched up the Rosebud until late on the twenty-fourth. His scouts returned with news that an Indian trail had been found, leading west into the valley of the Little Bighorn River. Subsequently, Custer ordered a forced march. There was no moon that night. Custer had intended that his column would cross the Wolf Mountains and then hide and rest for the day, June 25. If the camp was located, they would attack on the morning of June 26.

Well past midnight, Custer finally ordered a halt to rest his exhausted men and horses. Lieutenant Charles Varnum and several Crow scouts proceeded ahead, however. At dawn they climbed a high ridge south of Ash Creek known as the Crow's Nest. As the daylight brightened, through a field glass they were able to discern movement in the floodplain west of the Little Bighorn River. The scouts knew that the movement in the distance could only be a very large herd of horses.

Word was sent back to Custer, who immediately moved the column forward. Though he looked through the field glass, he was unable to see the horses his scouts insisted were there, so he decided there were probably no Indians anywhere in the valley. Later, however, when a sergeant reported seeing several Lakota riders behind them, Custer changed his mind. To Custer, however, the element of surprise had been lost. If there were Indians in the valley ahead, he was certain they were aware of his column, or would soon be. He immediately ordered his men to resume their march.

Custer moved east toward the Little Bighorn until about noon. Then he divided his regiment into three battalions. Three companies (H, K, and D) were assigned to Captain Frederick Benteen, the senior captain in the regiment and a frequent critic of his commanding officer. The second battalion (companies A, G, and M) was given to Major Marcus Reno, who also had his differences with Custer. Five companies (C, E, F, I, and L) composed the third battalion under Custer's direct command. Company C was commanded by Custer's younger brother, Captain Thomas Custer, and L, by Captain James Calhoun, his brother-in-law. The youngest of the Custer brothers, seventeen-year-old Boston, was also along; so was a nephew, Armstrong Reed.

B Company was assigned to guard the pack train, and it was essentially a fourth column after it had fallen behind.

Custer ordered Benteen to take his battalion southeast from Ash (now Reno) Creek to a line of bluffs several miles away, and attack any Indians he might find. If he found any, he was ordered to inform Custer immediately.

As Benteen departed, the Custer and Reno battalions followed Ash Creek west toward the Little Bighorn—Reno on the south bank and Custer on the north. The pack train with its 130 men was also on the north side, but it started to lag well behind. Near the south fork of Ash Creek, Custer gave Reno orders to proceed farther west, cross the Little Bighorn, find the camp if it was there, and attack. Captain Keogh, commander of I Company, and Custer's adjutant, Lieutenant W. W. Cooke, accompanied Reno to the crossing before they turned back. Somewhere after Reno's departure, Custer turned northward toward a line of ridges rising up from the eastern banks of the Little Bighorn River.

At that moment, Major General Alfred Terry and Colonel John Gibbon were waiting on the Yellowstone, Terry at the mouth of the Bighorn River, and Gibbon at Tullock's Creek, which flowed into the Bighorn. They were waiting for a message from Lieutenant Colonel George Custer that would apprise them of the reconnaissance of the lower part of Tullock's Creek.

Also at that moment, General George Crook was not too far south from the site of the battle he had fought eight days earlier. His men were hunting and fishing in the Big Horn Mountains.

Reno, of course, crossed the Little Bighorn south of its confluence with Ash Creek and wheeled right onto a broad floodplain. From there he took his column of tired men and horses northward, toward the southern end of the largest single encampment of Lakota ever seen on the northern plains.

TWELVE

The Aftermath Begins

FOR THE ENTIRE MONTH OF JULY, the army columns in the field from the Yellowstone River south did little or nothing effectively. Crook had been camped at Goose Creek, only a few miles from the site of the Rosebud Battle. Finally, on August 5, he started north toward the Rosebud, having been joined by none other than Buffalo Bill Cody. On August 8, Major General Terry also started up the Rosebud. Crook and Terry met without seeing a single Lakota.

Two weeks later, the combined force of nearly twenty-eight hundred soldiers separated. Terry reached the Yellowstone and turned east. Crook also headed generally east, once again disdaining the use of supply wagons, carrying his food and ammunition on pack mules. At one point he struggled through relentless rain that fell for days, and his horses succumbed to exhaustion and some even died. Food rations also gave out, forcing the soldiers to eat horse meat. Yet the column trudged on until it crossed into what is now North Dakota, on a line north of the Black Hills. There, turning south, Crook then crossed into what is now South Dakota. North of the Black Hills, at Slim Buttes, Crook found a target of opportunity and attacked the encampment of the Lakota headman American Horse.

That was the only success recorded by the U.S. Army for

the summer campaign, called the Yellowstone Expedition. The Powder River Expedition began in November. It was not as long or involved as the summer campaign had been, but it was more effective. Colonel Nelson Miles, new to the situation and the territory, and General Crook were spurred on by a white public unhappy about Custer's demise. Crook, determined to succeed, recruited and used dozens of Lakota and Cheyenne scouts.

On November 25, Colonel Ranald Mackenzie, under Crook's command, discovered Dull Knife's Cheyenne camp (northwest of the present town of Kaycee, Wyoming), and attacked it on a bitterly cold morning. The soldiers destroyed the village, but many of the Cheyenne escaped north to join Crazy Horse on the Tongue River.

Soon after, in early January of 1877, Miles's troops located Crazy Horse's encampment and attacked it. Crazy Horse and his warriors fought a series of running battles in the snow and cold, which enabled their women and children to escape. Still, the attack was a tactical victory for Miles because most of the Lakota's already meager winter supplies were destroyed. After that, though, Miles could not find Crazy Horse.

Crazy Horse and his followers endured a cold, hungry winter, bothered by the certainty that good weather would enable the soldiers to step up their attacks. He knew the consequences would be dire. Able-bodied fighting men with Crazy Horse numbered less than 130, and ammunition was scarce.

A month after Crazy Horse's fight with Miles, Sitting Bull and his followers fled to Canada, so Crazy Horse and his people were now alone. Crook, now at Camp Robinson, extended an olive branch to his former foe. He sent Lakota messengers to persuade Crazy Horse to surrender. Miles also wanted the prestige of bringing in Crazy Horse, but Crook had an advantage. Near Camp Robinson were the Spotted Tail and Red Cloud agencies, where friends and relatives of Crazy Horse had been living.

Crook sent Spotted Tail, Crazy Horse's uncle by marriage, to persuade him to surrender. Spotted Tail was the headman of the Sicangu Lakota, and he had an incomparable record as a fighting man as well as a reputation as a sensible leader. Those factors would not be ignored by Crazy Horse. But times had changed. At any given moment, Crook could pick someone else to be the chief at the Spotted Tail agency, whether it was named after him or not. Spotted Tail's position, if not his authority, flowed downward from the Indian agent. So it was not surprising that Spotted Tail made the arduous three-hundred-mile trek from Camp Robinson to the Tongue River region. And when he arrived, he promised—on behalf of Crook—that Crazy Horse would have his own agency in the Powder River country. But in fact, several delegations made the long trek from Camp Robinson to the Tongue River area, taking basically the same promise from Crook.

But no matter what Spotted Tail or the others said about the "good life" on the agencies, they did not persuade Crazy Horse to give in. Reality did. Buffalo were scarce, so the blankets and food promised by Crook were a powerful inducement.

There were no other viable options. He could have found a safe haven somewhere for the women and children and elderly, and then waged guerrilla war with his fighting men. But it would have been difficult to hide eight hundred people and ensure that they had enough to eat while the warriors were away. Ammunition was just as big an issue. In order to be an effective combat unit, Crazy Horse knew he and his men had to be *more* than adequately supplied with arms and ammunition. He was certainly tempted, but consideration for the safety and welfare of the helpless ones depended on his good judgment and overrode any thoughts of fighting it out to the last.

Crazy Horse was no fool. His decision to surrender had little to do with the prospect of any agency, and he had little faith in General Crook's promises, no matter who delivered them. His people were tired of running and needed to sleep without constant fear of attack. Crazy Horse decided that living under tough circumstances on an agency was better for his people, most of them women, children, and elderly, and better than death by starvation or from soldiers' bullets. So in early May of 1877, with a heavy heart he took his people to Camp Robinson.

By then, over one hundred winters had come and gone since that first group of belligerent Frenchman had swaggered up the Missouri River. Several years after that, a group of Sicangu Lakota hunting along the Missouri River found two starving white men digging up a cache of tallow, or fat. *Wasin icupi* (wah-shee ee-choo-be), they were dubbed—"they took the fat."

It is entirely likely that the Lakota word for whites—*wasicu* (wah-shee-chu)—evolved from that tongue-in-cheek description of two hungry white men. That thought goes through the mind of more than a few Lakota speakers each time the word is used.

Any opportunity, any secretly simmering hope for any kind of Lakota uprising, was destroyed when Crazy Horse was killed on September 5, 1877. The *wasicu* at Camp Robinson—from Crook on down—knew that Crazy Horse was the most capable military leader they had ever faced. If he were to lead an uprising, there would be all-out war. After all, it had not been that long since Crazy Horse had fought Crook to a standstill at Rosebud Creek.

So when a surly interpreter mistranslated Crazy Horse's words at a critical juncture, intentionally or unintentionally, paranoia overwhelmed reason. Crazy Horse's arrest was ordered, and a plan to ship him to the Dry Tortugas off the Florida coast went into high gear. But he would never see the inside of a Florida prison. He physically resisted the attempt to incarcerate him, and in the ensuing chaos and confusion, a soldier with a bayonet stabbed him through both kidneys.

Though Sitting Bull returned from Canada in 1881, he was an older man, and too cautious to be the threat he once had been. There would be one last desperate attempt by the Lakota to fight back, but with Crazy Horse gone and Sitting Bull ineffectual, the *wasicu* found themselves in full and total control.

THIRTEEN

Into the Shadows

LAKOTA RESISTANCE to white encroachment essentially ended when Crazy Horse handed over his rifle to an army officer at Camp Robinson in May of 1877. Though there were minor outbursts over the next few years, the last angry armed resistance would flare up briefly at Wounded Knee Creek in the latter part of December of 1890. From September of 1877 to early 1890, a shadow fell heavily on the land, quelling the Lakota spirit like rain dousing a campfire. Even history seems to have turned its back on those years, since very little is said or written about the years from 1877 to 1889. For those years, the hopes, dreams, and vitality of our Lakota ancestors were probably at the lowest they have ever been. But the Earth kept spinning during those years, and things did happen.

Jealousy and suspicion

UNREST HAD BEEN SIMMERING on the Red Cloud and Spotted Tail agencies for several years. No Lakota could have imagined how life would be while living under the control of the whites, and nothing prepared anyone for the reality of it. A loss of dignity came on the heels of loss of freedom. People who once felt their spirits expand because they knew their lands went far beyond the horizon now felt their spirits shrink within the incredibly small physical boundaries imposed upon them. Ten years before, a man would have needed a good horse and thirty to forty days to traverse the length or breadth of the nation, whether it was from the Great Muddy (Missouri) River to the Shining (Big Horn) Mountains, or from the Shell (North Platte) River north to the Elk (Yellowstone) River. Now even the oldest horse could travel across the agencies in a day, or sometimes less. Lakota lands no longer reached to the far horizons. It was no wonder that anger roiled in a man's chest like a restless bear.

There were other less apparent differences, but changes no less difficult to live with. Now any man who wanted to lead had to curry favor from the whites. It was no longer possible to distinguish oneself by one's own deeds or courage. This was exceedingly bitter medicine to swallow. Not long after Crazy Horse and his people arrived, some of the army officers and Indian Bureau subagents talked of making him the overall chief of all the Lakota on the agencies. He, of course, was expecting that he and his band would return to the Powder River country to their own agency. So any talk of making him "chief" was irrelevant nonsense to him, but not to others who might lose their power if he was made chief. Adding to the tension was the whites' fear that Crazy Horse might lead restless young men to break out of the agency.

To his credit, Crook attempted to make a separate agency for Crazy Horse a reality, but the U.S. government was not prepared to stand behind the general's promise to a subjugated Lakota leader, especially one who had embarrassed them twice. When a half-breed interpreter mistranslated Crazy Horse's answer to a question, rumors about Crazy Horse's true allegiance fueled paranoia. Though Crook did not give in to the rumors initially, he was eventually convinced that Crazy Horse intended to do him harm. He ordered his arrest soon after.

While resisting incarceration, Crazy Horse was killed on September 5, 1877. For the army and the U.S. government, the threat of an uprising had been thwarted. But many Lakota believe he was murdered. His death might have been a consequence of the jealousy of a Lakota who wanted him out of the way. On the other hand, it is also possible that a careful plan was contrived to use the infighting among the Lakota as a vehicle to squash the last chance for an uprising. Either way, two facts are unavoidable: Many of Crazy Horse's own people were jealous of him; and among the whites in the Indian Bureau and the army, many were convinced that Crazy Horse could, and would, lead an armed uprising. To them, sending him away to a prison off the Florida coast was a logical response. We will probably never know the whole truth.

Old lands, new ways

THE DEATH OF CRAZY HORSE was the final blow to the Lakota spirit, especially for his supporters. White civilian and military authorities held their breath, fearing retribution. But when the greatest warrior among the Lakota was killed, so was the fire of resistance.

Several weeks later, the Lakota were moved north. The boundaries of the 1868 Fort Laramie Treaty had been erased and the "unceded lands" ceased to exist. That left only the eastern two thirds of the Great Sioux Reservation for them to live on. The "Agreement" of 1875 had taken the western third, that portion containing the gold-rich Black Hills.

Terminology changed with the new situation. The word *reservation* replaced the word *agency*. Agencies now were the towns where the Indian Agent was headquartered. The Lakota called the agencies *owakpamni* (oh-wah-kpah-mnee), meaning a "place of distribution," a name indicative of the new lifestyle. Agencies were the sites for distribution of annuities, which was mainly food.

The agent was called *ateyapi* (ah-teh-yah-be), meaning "we use for a father." Over time there would be distribution substations on the reservations where subagents were assigned and often lived. In English they were "boss farmers," because it was their responsibility to teach nomadic hunters how to farm. Their Lakota title was *owoju wicasa* (oh-woh-ju we-cha-sha), or "man who plants."

With the distribution of food at issue stations came a strange little tradition. Live cattle, usually longhorns, were brought in to fulfill the food annuity. Lakota men were offered a rifle with one bullet and the privilege of shooting an animal themselves. It was a pitiful reminder of a time when they hunted buffalo from the backs of their horses.

The Lakota scattered over their reservations and tried to make a new life for themselves. Even though they walked over familiar landscapes where the seasons came and went, rivers flowed, and the sun still rose and set as it always had, there was no way to shake off the reality of change. The whites had prevailed, and surviving among them—and in spite of them—was the new reality. But there were more difficult changes to be faced.

The policy of assimilation hit with full force.

Short hair and tight shoes

A NUMBER OF LAKOTA CHILDREN were unwillingly taken from their families. The purveyors of assimilation turned a deaf ear and a cold heart to cries of protest, having determined that "killing the Indian and saving the man" was in the best interests of everyone involved. One notable parent allowed several of his children to be taken east to the newly established Carlisle Industrial School for Indians, in Carlisle, Pennsylvania.

Spotted Tail, of the Sicangu, had long advocated that the Lakota should change their ways, and he was willing to put his children in the forefront. But though he might have acquiesced to the idea of a white man's education, he apparently did not like their methodology. During a visit to Carlisle, he was angered over the heavy-handed treatment his children described. Their hair had been cut severely short, and many other children complained that the leather shoes they were given were too stiff and tight. They were made to stand in line and march in line, and they were physically punished for speaking their native languages.

Spotted Tail took his children home over the objections of the school's superintendent, Captain Henry Pratt. But not all the native children at Carlisle, or any other boarding school, would be as fortunate as Spotted Tail's children. Many had to endure years away from home and family as well as the strict and regimented lifestyle enforced at those institutions. Administrators, teachers, and dormitory matrons carried out the policy and the process of assimilation with impunity.

Carlisle was funded and operated by the U.S. government, and it realized that the job of civilizing so many native children would be extremely costly. Churches were enlisted to help, and many were only too glad to lend a hand. The prospect of converting so many souls to Christianity was appealing. The government granted sections of tribal land (a section is 640 acres) on which parochial boarding schools could be built and operated. Not only were the schools given land, they were also given the authority to take native children from their homes if their parents did not willingly let them attend school.

All in all, the process of assimilation was intended to destroy native culture by stopping its growth in the young. The premise was based on how America thought of itself, articulated by Judge Elmer Dundy's opinion in his decision in *Standing Bear v. Crook* in 1879, part of which stated:

> On one side we have the remnants of a once numerous and powerful, but now weak, insignificant, unlettered, and generally despised race. On the other, we have the representatives of one of the most powerful, most enlightened, and most christianized nations of modern times . . .

Since America thought so well of itself, it was only logical that all "weak, insignificant, unlettered, and generally despised" people should be forced to fit the mold. Therefore, it was worth inflicting physical and emotional pain on native children.

Spotted Tail, of course, had a different take on the issue. He saw education as a way for his children to live more easily in the white man's world. He was wise enough to realize that the rules of survival had changed, and he wanted Lakota children to survive. Adjusting to a different lifestyle was necessary. Having to give up the core of one's identity to do it, in Spotted Tail's view, was not necessary.

The last hunt

TO SMOOTH Spotted Tail's ruffled feathers, the Indian Bureau built a large frame house for him, on a low bluff near the Rosebud Agency. This raised the ire of one of his opponents and harshest critics, Crow Dog, who already believed that Spotted Tail was selling Lakota land to the railroads. In November of 1881, Crow Dog shot and killed Spotted Tail. With his death ended one of the longest tenures of leadership among any of the Lakota bands. (Crow Dog was arrested, tried, and convicted, although the Spotted Tail and Crow Dog families agreed on a payment to settle the issue. Later, the U.S. Supreme Court overturned the conviction because the court lacked jurisdiction over Crow Dog.) Though there were other leaders among the Lakota, such as Swift Bear, none had Spotted Tail's stature with the Indian agent, so the Sicangu no longer had the ear of the U.S. government.

The same year Spotted Tail was killed, Sitting Bull returned from Canada. After the government incarcerated him and a few followers at Fort Randall, in what is now southeast South Dakota, he inexplicably joined Buffalo Bill's Wild West Show for one season. Then he took up residence along the Grand River on the Standing Rock Reservation (in present-day north central South Dakota and south central North Dakota). In 1883, a herd of several hundred buffalo were discovered north of the Black Hills, probably survivors of one of the last concentrated hunts by white hide hunters. Sitting Bull and his people found the herd south of the Grand River, and killed them all. Understandably, buffalo meat was much preferable to the lean longhorns provided by the Indian Bureau. But in a strange twist of irony, the Lakota probably wiped out the last large wild herd on the northern plains.

As the years went by, Sitting Bull was more and more inclined to stay on the reservation, eventually pointedly staying away from the reservation's agency headquarters at Fort Yates.

By now the Great Sioux Reservation had lost its 1868 configuration, and the geographic identities of several smaller reservations emerged, much as we know them today.

The Oglala and Sicangu reservations were adjacent to each other just north of the current border between Nebraska and South Dakota. They were now called the Pine Ridge and Rosebud Sioux, respectively. In the northeastern portion of what was once the Great Sioux Reservation were the other five bands. The Mniconju were on the Cheyenne River Reservation, west of the current state capital and west of the Missouri River. North and adjacent to them were the Hunkpapa on the Standing Rock Reservation, with nearly half of its boundaries into the current state of North Dakota. Interspersed on both reservations were the smaller bands of Itazipacola, Oohenunpa, and Sihasapa.

Three crucial events occurred in the late 1880s that would dramatically affect the Lakota. One would have an immediate impact and consequences, and the fallout from the other two is still with us today.

The first occurred in 1887, when the United States Congress passed the Dawes Severalty Act, or General Allotment Act—also called the Homestead Act. Until then, the lands within the exterior borders of each of the newly established reservations were owned collectively by the tribe. Dawes mandated that the land be surveyed and subdivided, and all males eighteen years and older be counted. That was the allotment portion affecting the Lakota. The homestead portion of the act would benefit whites. Though the implementation of the act was ponderously slow, its effect was catastrophic nonetheless.

If the Lakota thought that the cessation of military hostilities was the end of conflict for them, they were wrong. By the time most of them realized that what was left of the Great Sioux Reservation was a larger area than the original agencies in northwest Nebraska, the United States further divided that tract into separate reservations. Most were unaware that the Dawes Act had been passed, but they would certainly live with its impact later. Everyone, except for those born on the agencies from the late 1860s on, knew that they had lost something they could never recover. In short, the freedom to move as often and far as they wanted was prohibited by boundaries. Some who tested those boundaries were pursued and apprehended by soldiers. The reality of the new order was hardest on those who had lived the free-roaming nomadic lifestyle. It is no wonder that some would reach for a shred of hope carried on the swirling winds of change.

The last hope

THE SECOND EVENT occurred in northern Nevada in 1888, when a Paiute Indian had a vision during a solar eclipse. Wovoka was his name, at least the name history would know him by. He was a still a young man when he had his vision "when the sun died," in 1888. His beliefs were a mixture of Paiute and Christianity, probably because a white family raised him after his father had died. That was not an unusual circumstance in those times, but the message he began preaching was.

God told him in a vision, he reported, that Indians should turn away from war and learn to live peacefully with whites. But more important, the earth could be healed and returned to the Indians. Even dead relatives and ancestors could be brought back. To accomplish this, Indians would have to perform a special dance God had given to Wovoka.

Wovoka's message could not have come at a more vulnerable moment. His own Paiute people were the first to believe his message, and they danced. Then they shared the message with other peoples. Utes, Shoshones, Cheyenne, and Arapaho all listened. Many believed and began dancing to change the world. Because its purpose was to bring back dead relatives and ancestors, it became known as the Ghost Dance. Women danced along with men, fervently believing that faith and effort would bring the desired result. Many people danced continuously, often until they went into a trance. Some reported seeing dead relatives. This, of course, inspired others to participate. Songs that articulated the desperation felt by all native peoples were composed and sung.

The Ghost Dance spread quickly, especially in the Southwest and the northern plains. From the beginning, whites were fearful, assuming it was a war dance. But, of course, there was no thought to making war because the dance was the way to change everything without war.

The third crucial event happened in the middle of all the anxiety and activity over the Ghost Dance. A legal shift occurred, and Dakota Territory was divided in half and became the states of North Dakota and South Dakota. At the time, the new status was important only to the white citizens of the new states. But it was important to the Lakota also, and the full implication of statehood would have an impact later, when the core of their sovereignty as a native nation was attacked. Furthermore, statehood helped to increase the effect of the Dawes Act. Because Dawes had individualized ownership of Indian land, some Lakota landowners eventually did sell land to white farmers and ranches. Those portions of land would then be subject to *state* civil and criminal jurisdiction.

Lakota delegates were sent to hear Wovoka's message and returned in the spring of 1890 after several months. The Pine Ridge Indian agent promptly threw them in the stockade, hoping to stem the growth of the new religion before it could take root. But it was too late. Rumors carrying the basic message of the Ghost Dance—straws of hope floating on the winds of change—had already reached the Lakota reservations.

Exacerbating an already delicate situation, the U.S. Congress cut the beef rations at both the Pine Ridge and Rosebud reservations. No government official, from the agency level to the commissioner of the Bureau of Indian Affairs, had considered that sweetening the pot, as it were, with a timely delivery of extra food rations would have been taken as a gesture of compassion and generosity. To make matters worse, a drought gripped the land, and localized epidemics of whooping cough, influenza, and measles killed people, adding to the misery.

So the Lakota flocked to the Ghost Dance.

Driven by desperation and defiance, the Lakota, especially on the Pine Ridge Reservation, performed the dance openly. But it was known that hundreds, if not thousands, of Lakota on four reservations were involved in the movement. The movement was escalating, with many people performing the dance out of sight of any whites.

In a classic act of self-preservation, the Indian Agent at Pine Ridge resigned in October, solving his problem by removing himself from it. Keeping its record of ineptitude quite intact, the government appointed a replacement by the name of Daniel Royer—clearly a political appointment. Royer could not have been less suited for the position. Shortly after he took the job, he declared the situation out of control. It was out of his control, to be sure.

Somewhere in the process, Agent Royer must have heard that some of the Ghost Dancers had added a twist unique to the Lakota. They made and wore Ghost Shirts during the dance, believing them to be protection against bullets. No uprisings were being planned. The Ghost Shirts were protection in the event Indian police or soldiers attacked the dancers.

Learning about the Ghost Shirts, whites on or near the reservations relayed their fears of a military uprising to the U.S. government. Why would Ghost Dancers wear bulletproof shirts unless they had plans to attack someone?

Long knives and iron breasts

BY NOW AGENT ROYER was sending daily telegrams requesting federal troops. Their presence in great numbers, he advised, was the only solution to the growing problem. Someone listened to the panic-stricken agent, who had been named by the Lakota Koskalaka Lakota Kowicakpe, or "Young Man Afraid of Lakota." Young Man Afraid of Lakota got his wish. The U.S. government transferred jurisdiction of the reservations from the Department of the Interior to the Department of War. Within a matter of days, nearly three thousand troops were in the field, most of them in and around Pine Ridge. One of the units was the U.S. Seventh Cavalry, now under the command of Colonel James Forsyth.

If the intent and the purpose of the military was to restore order to the so-called unrest on the reservations, they failed, instigating fear instead. Fear of them. Ghost Dancers from the Pine Ridge and Rosebud reservations fled in droves to the Badlands, a region of eroded landscapes adjacent to the northwest corner of the Pine Ridge Reservation. The Badlands were a maze of canyons and plateaus, a perfect hiding place. In short order, over a thousand people were hiding out there. The army, of course, declared them to be "hostiles."

Troop presence in such strength chased the Ghost Dancing underground, especially on the Pine Ridge and Rosebud reservations. To military authorities dealing in tangibles, no obvious dancing meant that it had been significantly curtailed, or stopped. On the Standing Rock and Cheyenne River reservations, where there were fewer troops, people were still dancing openly, especially at the camp of an old headman named Big Foot, a Mniconju.

At this juncture, the Indian Bureau turned over to the army a list of names of "troublemakers" to be arrested—individuals who, in the government's view, had been the cause of all their troubles. Less than twenty names, combined, were turned in by the Indian agents of Rosebud, Standing Rock, and Cheyenne River. Agent Royer, of the Pine Ridge Agency, turned in more than fifty names, a conservative estimate, in his words.

Immediately after the army took jurisdiction of the reservations, a plan was already in motion to arrest Sitting Bull, using his erstwhile friend Buffalo Bill Cody to persuade the Hunkpapa leader to turn himself in. The army assumed that Sitting Bull was heavily involved with the Ghost Dance and therefore a dangerous influence. Agent James McLaughlin at Standing Rock, however, put a stop to that grandiose plan. Though Cody did arrive at Fort

Yates, on the Standing Rock, in late November, the trip was nothing more than a sightseeing tour.

McLaughlin's reasoning had nothing remotely to do with Sitting Bull's welfare, however. He wanted his own Indian police—Hunkpapa and Mniconju Lakota—who had been trained as such, to make the arrest. The agent felt that Indian police would arouse less suspicion than soldiers. He might have been right, but to most Lakota a blue uniform was a blue uniform, and no matter who wore it, it symbolized the heavy-handed authority of the U. S. government. The Lakota had a variety of names for the Indian police. *Wawoyuspe* (wah-woh-you-speh) was one of the first, meaning, literally, "one who catches," because Indian police apprehended and arrested people. *Canksa yuha* (chan-ksah you-hah) was another, meaning "has a short stick," in reference to the wooden clubs carried by most Indian police. *Maku maza* (mah-coo mah-zah) was in reference to the badges and meant "iron breast."

Agent McLaughlin and the military commander at Fort Yates finally concurred that the arrest would be made on December 20, issue day at the agency. Many of Sitting Bull's immediate followers would be collecting rations, leaving only a few with the headman. But McLaughlin and his Indian police had to change the plan. They were informed that Sitting Bull was leaving for Pine Ridge. That information was not credible, but McLaughlin had to accept it at face value. By the evening of December 14, just over forty Indian police and a hundred-man detachment of cavalry were deployed.

At dawn the following morning, December 15, the Indian police, under the command of Lieutenant Henry Bullhead, had surrounded Sitting Bull's small log house. The cavalry waited a few miles away, ready to provide support if and when necessary.

FOURTEEN

At Wounded Knee

VIOLENT DEATH was the U.S. government's solution to the Ghost Dance in 1890. Within a span of fourteen days at the beginning of a winter that will never be forgotten, some three hundred Lakota were killed. The guns of soldiers did the deed, but it was the irrationality of blind fear that set the stage.

In the middle of November, Agent Daniel Royer had sent a telegram to Washington. It read:

> Indians are dancing in the snow and are wild and crazy. I have fully informed you that employes [sic] and government property at this agency have no protection and are at the mercy of these dancers. Why delay further investigation? We need protection, and we need it now. The leaders should be arrested and confined in some military post until the matter is quieted, and this should be done at once.

Sitting Bull

INDIAN POLICEMEN had been a fact of life on many reservations throughout the West. Whites viewed them as progressive, but the reaction was mixed in the Lakota communities. Men like Sitting Bull were suspicious of any Lakota who worked for the whites. Lieutenant Henry Bullhead was one of those policemen, and he was a Hunkpapa Lakota.

Lieutenant Bullhead and his police contingent of just over forty men approached Sitting Bull's compound at dawn. Bullhead unceremoniously entered Sitting Bull's house and announced that he was being taken prisoner. Sitting Bull emerged from his house calmly, but then scolded the younger Bullhead for his discourtesy. An angry crowd had gathered after the police arrived, and among them was Sitting Bull's son. The young man—only seventeen years old—berated his father for allowing the situation to occur.

The sight of their beloved leader in the custody of anyone in a blue uniform was unacceptable to many in the crowd. Threats were shouted. As the police tried to push their way through, Sitting Bull called out. Someone in the crowd fired a gun, striking Lieutenant Bullhead. As he was falling, Bullhead shot Sitting Bull. Sergeant Red Tomahawk, walking behind both of them, shot the sagging and already mortally wounded Sitting Bull through the back of the head.

An exchange of gunfire and a vicious, hand-to-hand melee ensued. Though the Sitting Bull supporters outnumbered the police, they were outgunned. If not for light artillery fire from the troops a short distance from the camp, the police contingent might all have been killed. As it was, six policemen were killed or wounded. Sitting Bull, his young son, and six others from his camp were killed. Agent McLaughlin's Lakota police, as catalysts for the government, eliminated Sitting Bull, the object of McLaughlin's fear and loathing. McLaughlin had described Sitting Bull as the "leading apostle of this latest Indian absurdity." Though Sitting Bull had not fully endorsed the Ghost Dance, neither did he completely dismiss it. He saw it for what it was—a gesture of desperation and a phase that would eventually pass.

But the misunderstandings continued. General Nelson Miles had responded to Agent Royer's request and ordered troops to Pine Ridge, thinking that a show of overwhelming force would prevent conflict. Consequently, many of the Ghost Dancers fled to the Badlands, certain that the presence of so many troops could mean nothing good. Though Miles may have sincerely thought that a show of force would be sufficient to avoid bloodshed, his desire to avoid conflict did not coincide with the methodology. He was thinking like a soldier with power at his beck and call, not a peacemaker trying to use reason.

Word of Sitting Bull's death spread, and the immediate conclusion among most Lakota was murder. Thirteen years earlier, the same government had plans to seize Crazy Horse and send him to the Dry Tortugas off the Florida Keys. To most Lakota, the consequences of the U.S. government's attempts to arrest and apprehend Crazy Horse in 1877 and Sitting Bull in 1890 were frighteningly similar. The two most influential and powerful Lakota leaders of the nineteenth century dying violently at the hands of U.S. soldiers and agency police could not be dismissed as coincidence. Tragically, the death of Sitting Bull and several of his people on December 15 was only the beginning.

Big Foot

OTHER ARRESTS were planned, with paranoia doing the planning. The next likely troublemaker, according to the U.S. government, was an old headman named Big Foot, a Mniconju. He was encamped along the Cheyenne River under the watchful eyes of Lieutenant Colonel E. V. Sumner and one company of the Seventh Cavalry. A few dozen people fleeing from Sitting Bull's camp joined Big Foot, destitute and still in shock over the death of their leader. Big Foot himself was ill, but the newcomers were Sitting Bull's people, and that was enough for Sumner to suspect Big Foot of some kind of mischief. Sumner sent a request for reinforcements and informed Big Foot that he and his people would be escorted under arrest to the agency at Fort Yates. Before more troops arrived, however, Big Foot and his ragged band of mostly women and children bolted for the safety of the Badlands, a little less than a hundred miles to the south.

The last thing on Big Foot's mind was any kind of armed resistance. He was trying desperately to hide his people from the soldiers. There was no reason for any Lakota to trust them, especially after the death of Sitting Bull. Furthermore, thousands of troops had been on and around the reservations for weeks. Many of them were pushing in from the north and west of the Badlands, forcing out the Lakota hiding there south toward Pine Ridge. In spite of reassurances from the general in charge, John Brooke, that he would protect anyone who surrendered peaceably, the Lakota were justifiably skeptical. But they had little choice. They were ill equipped for winter and poorly armed.

When Big Foot entered the Badlands, he found no one. He had no way of knowing, of course, that many of the beleaguered Ghost Dancers had given up the dance, and turned themselves in at Pine Ridge. The possible consequences from the increasing presence of army troops was too frightening. By now, Big Foot's illness had progressed to full-blown pneumonia. Sanctuary at Pine Ridge under whatever protection the old headman Red

Cloud could offer seemed the only course available. But it was not to be.

Wounded Knee Creek

ON DECEMBER 28, Big Foot, now lying on drag poles behind a horse because he was too ill to ride or walk, was told that four companies of the U.S. Seventh Cavalry had caught up with them. The commander, Major Samuel Whitside, demanded unconditional surrender, and Big Foot did not argue. He and his people were then escorted to a small settlement of sorts near Wounded Knee Creek, fifteen miles east of the Pine Ridge Reservation. There, four more companies and the overall commander of the Seventh, Colonel Forsyth, also arrived.

The eight companies, plus a few scouts, numbered nearly five hundred men. They had with them four Hotchkiss guns, which were state of the art, rapid-fire light artillery that fired two-inch, high-explosive shells.

Big Foot and his followers encamped south of a low plateau. They numbered approximately 350 cold, hungry, and tired people. On the plateau above them were the Hotchkiss guns.

Colonel Forsyth sent a small stove for Big Foot's tent, along with his regimental surgeon to give whatever aid he could to the ailing man. At the same time, he positioned his soldiers around Big Foot's camp to keep order.

The next morning, the men of Big Foot's contingent gathered north of the camp. Forsyth wasted no time in instructing them to surrender their weapons. But the first groups tossed down only a few antiquated guns. This was not quite the level of cooperation Forsyth wanted.

Big Foot's people were outnumbered overall by their captors. But the men—the fighters—were outnumbered a staggering five to one. That fact alone made the Lakota nervous and
apprehensive. Now the odds against them would increase even
more because the soldiers wanted Lakota weapons. What would
happen after the Lakota surrendered their weapons was any-
body's guess. And no one among the Lakota was convinced that
the white flag of truce flying in their camp meant anything to the
soldiers.

Fourteen days had passed since Sitting Bull had been killed.
That sad fact hung over the proceedings as well, stirring a myr-
iad of emotions, including disbelief and anger. Then the soldiers
positioned near the men were ordered to do a lodge-by-lodge
search. Here is where the foundation for what followed later was
laid.

The soldiers burst into lodge after lodge, kicking and throwing aside furnishings and personal items. Women were shoved
aside, some pushed to the ground, their protests ignored. The
further the search progressed among the lodges, the worse the
situation became. Women and children called out to their husbands and fathers, whose agitation escalated into anger with each
shout and scream from the village.

Had the soldiers tempered their approach and conducted
themselves with restraint, the women would still have been unhappy with the search, but a slow and deliberate manner would
not have ignited the Lakotas' anxiety into smoldering anger. After all, the soldiers were in control of the situation, and they had
the tactical advantage with superior numbers and more weapons.
For that matter, Colonel Forsyth, who had demonstrated a capa-
bility for kindness by his gesture to Big Foot the night before,

could have halted the search and instructed his soldiers not to be so heavy-handed. But he did not, and soon the opportunity to calm the situation passed.

Cries of protest and anguish continued until the invasive search was completed. In the end, fewer than fifty weapons were collected. By now, the Lakota men were on the razor's edge of anger. A medicine man reminded some of them they were wearing Ghost Shirts that would protect them from the soldiers' bullets. Forsyth, or any of the soldiers close by, could not understand the man's words.

The exact, single incident that finally incited gunfire has been long debated. White historians cling to the story that an angry young Lakota man with a gun was the instigator. Government authorities even went so far as to produce a Lakota witness to attest to this allegation. The young man reportedly pulled out his weapon and killed a soldier.

On the Lakota side, a sad misunderstanding led to the tragedy. The young man was deaf and was keeping a rifle beneath his blanket because he could not fully comprehend what was happening. When he saw weapons being thrown on the ground, he grabbed his too—perhaps thinking to give it up, or maybe intending to use it. But he never got the opportunity to carry out his intent. A soldier grappled with him, and the rifle went off during the struggle. It is enough to say that however it happened, a shot was fired.

Upon hearing the shot, the soldiers opened fire with their .50-caliber rifles at point-blank range.

The Lakota men, who had convened north of the camp, took heavy casualties from the first volley. Half or more of the hundred fell, Big Foot among them. Others pulled out concealed knives or war clubs and attacked. Slashing and swinging, they waded into the nearest soldiers. The vicious hand-to-hand fighting continued even as the Hotchkiss guns opened fire. By now, the outer ring of soldiers also opened fire with their rifles. Those on the west, south, and east fired into the camp, targeting women and children. As did the Hotchkiss guns. The outer ring of soldiers also began shooting at women and children who had sought shelter in the dry ravine south of the camp at the first sounds of gunfire, and then began to flee as the firing increased. Soldiers still in the camp were killed by their comrades, as many as twenty-six. Within scant minutes, two hundred Lakota were killed. Lodges in the camp were shattered by the high-explosive artillery shells. Then the Hotchkiss guns were moved to enable better coverage of the ravine, their shells bursting among the fleeing women and children. The muzzle blasts of the artillery and the explosions of their shells could be heard in Pine Ridge, some fifteen miles away.

Soldiers took up the pursuit in the ravine, yet some of the women and children managed to make it over a mile from camp before they were cut down. All along the path of panicked flight, bodies were strewn in a long line. Many of the dead women had shawls or blankets over their faces, sometimes with a child inside, as if trying to hide from the inevitable blast of a soldier's gun, pointing from only a few feet away. A few, only a few, found places to hide.

There was one final insult, an act that affirmed the mind-set of those behind the guns on this unspeakable day. After the murderous firing finally abated, soldiers and scouts searched along the dry ravine and beyond, looking for survivors who had somehow found places to hide. A group of young boys were lured into the open by soldiers, only to be riddled with bullets.

Several Lakota who had come in from the Badlands to the agency several days earlier heard the firing. They rode out, and near Wounded Knee they found soldiers searching in the gullies and brush for survivors, and then they attacked them. The soldiers retreated to their main body, and the attackers could do nothing more. They watched from a distance as the soldiers gathered up their own dead and wounded as well as a few dozen Lakota prisoners—all of them wounded—and moved out toward the agency.

No one counted the Lakota dead, but the number was likely nearly three hundred—and mostly women and children. The bodies were frozen by a blizzard that rolled in several hours after the guns had fallen silent.

A burial detachment was sent out on January 1, 1891. Civilians were paid two dollars per body. A long trench was dug in the cold ground and frozen bodies were unceremoniously pushed or rolled in. Some, those wearing Ghost Shirts or dresses, had been stripped naked. If anyone paused in silence or uttered a prayer, no one knows. Photographs were taken, and many were of the frozen bodies before burial.

There was somewhat of a knee-jerk reaction, perhaps from a righteous sense of outrage. A large contingent of former Ghost Dancers, lately in from the Badlands, took to the field, attacking soldiers and supply wagons. But as quickly as their brief campaign was organized, it fell apart.

In dramatic fashion, the Ghost Dance was over. General Miles brought all available troops to Pine Ridge, completely surrounding the agency until all hostilities ceased. On January 16, 1891, the leaders of the last final outbreaks surrendered.

Thus the war to repel white invasion ended.

In the silence

IN THE IMMEDIATE MOMENTS after the deafening blasts of artillery and rifle fire had stopped, the silence must have been utterly profound. The world has known far too many moments such as that, when the killing mercifully ends.

There was no victory at Wounded Knee for either the Lakota or the soldiers. We can only wonder if there was a sense of accomplishment for those who were still standing with guns in their hands when the silence descended. One can only hope that among the four hundred soldiers who survived, even a few truly felt the depth and enormity of the inhumanity they had committed. Even a little remorse hints that some shred of compassion has survived, and therein lies the hope for us all.

Yet someone had to have seen Wounded Knee as a worthy act on some level. Eighteen Medals of Honor were awarded to the soldiers of the Seventh Cavalry. How can anyone be decorated for bravery or for commitment to duty when killing defenseless women and children?

Takuwe. Why?

That question will always echo with the hollowness of anguish.

Now and then, someone whispers that Captains Edgerly, Godfrey, Moylan, Wallace, and Varnum had been at the Little Bighorn fourteen years earlier. They had to have remembered and described the sting of that defeat. And there, in that ragtag village along Wounded Knee Creek, were people of the nation that had so soundly whipped them. Surely, the thought of revenge had to have been rekindled by someone wearing a uniform.

Nothing can change what happened at Wounded Knee. Nothing can change that turbulent history, or bring back Sitting Bull, or satisfactorily explain why it happened the way it did.

So we should all weep, no matter if our ancestors wore uniforms or fled for their lives on that day. And when the weeping ends, in the silence that follows, we must vow never to forget, no matter how painful. For it is in the remembering that we may find an answer, one that may prevent Wounded Knee from happening again.

FIFTEEN

Possibilities

THE SEEDS OF CHANGE for the Lakota were deeply implanted early in the eighteenth century with the contentious journey of the La Vérendrye party up the Missouri River. During the following decades, the Missouri became an important passage for commerce. Initial contacts between whites and natives along the river were friendly for the most part. But if there had been conflict and early resistance, our history would be much the same. The only consequence of early resistance would have been to impede the arrival of whites for only a few decades more. The die had been irrevocably cast because the members of a race that had inundated the lands and overwhelmed the native peoples east of the Mississippi River had laid eyes on this new and vast frontier. Obviously, they could not see the entire length and breadth of it, but they did not need to. Theirs was a far more inclusive glimpse. They saw possibilities.

A different road

WOUNDED KNEE was a devastating blow to the spirit of the Lakota people. There were no more significant armed clashes. If there were any further thoughts of resistance, they were spoken in cautious whispers. The U.S. miliary had demonstrated how far it was willing and able to go to subjugate the Lakota. Some second-guessing understandably occurred. Interspersed liberally in those conversations was the phrase *ktat ka*, meaning essentially "if only." *Hecunqunpi ktat ka.* "If only we had done it that way." It was part of the grieving process.

No matter the clarity of hindsight, the harsh reality of life in 1891 could not be avoided. The self-confident stare of a people who had watched the La Vérendryes and the wagons on the Holy Road had turned blank. Now they gazed forlornly into meager fires and empty pots. There was nothing to do but mourn the old days and face each day and survive it. That was the immediate and constant challenge.

Survival now required the patience to endure inactivity. In the old days, the women would comment in passing that the food containers were nearly empty. In response the men would take up their weapons to hunt. Now the women said nothing because it was the whims and policies of the U.S. government that filled the food containers, or kept them empty. Hunting now amounted to standing in line on issue day for meager rations.

Survival was dependent on adaptability. The ability to change and adapt was one reason the first groups of Lakota were able to survive and thrive on the plains. After Wounded Knee, it seemed there was little choice but to change, and in a hurry. But as a matter of fact, some change had already been happening.

From the start of consistent trade with whites, items necessary for everyday family life were highly coveted, such as iron cooking pots, tin plates and cups, knives, wool blankets, needles, and trade cloth, to list a few. Over the decades those types of items became part of Lakota households, and their precontact versions became obsolete. It was unusual, for example, for children born after 1850 to see anyone making an obsidian knife.

After two generations, the knowledge for making stone knives still existed, but the skill and ability to do so began to diminish because no one made them consistently. The handing down of these kinds of skills did not just wither away unnoticed, however. It was a process of choice, not of coercion.

By the early 1880s, most Lakota were making clothing out of cloth, especially calico or muslin, or were wearing white-manufactured clothing. It was convenient but also necessary because the traditional raw materials—elk, deer, bison, and antelope hides—were no longer readily available. Cloth dresses and shirts were cut to traditional patterns, however, and for a time both men's and women's leggings were made from trade cloth or wool blankets. By 1890, that trend had diminished and Euro-American clothing was worn more and more. Understandably, however, it is much easier to adopt the *things* of another culture. While our ancestors liked, wanted, and used clothing, tools, utensils, firearms, and oil lamps, they could not take on the *ways* of the whites as easily.

While some cultural icons were easily discarded—such as stone arrowheads—the Lakota hung on to one of the strongest symbols of their culture and lifestyle—the *tipestola*, or "pointed dwelling," the tipi. The people who had given in to the agencies in the late 1860s (initially) gave up their guns and horses, but not their dwellings. They did not have to, and they probably saved the Indian Bureau hundreds of thousands of dollars because it did not have to construct houses. Consequently, the tipi became an unavoidable necessity. The government had built a large frame house for Spotted Tail near the Rosebud Agency, but he preferred the open air and the amenities of the tipi. And

Sitting Bull, who slept in a log house on the Standing Rock reservation, also much preferred the tipi.

The tipi enabled the Lakota to remain mobile, even in those last difficult months leading to Wounded Knee. If nothing else, they had shelter for the night even if there was no meat in the kettle. Mobility was also still very important. With tipis they could run from trouble and easily take their shelter with them. By the 1880s, more and more tipis were made of canvas because buffalo hides simply were not available for repair or for new tipi coverings. Also on the scene were canvas wall tents acquired in trade. They were convenient to mobility as well. But in spite of their loyalty to the tipi, by the early 1880s the Lakota were beginning to live in log cabins, and by the middle of that decade they had proliferated on all the reservations.

After Wounded Knee, however, defeated people gazed over the far horizons only to recall better times and old trails they could no longer follow. Now their longest treks were to the agency issue houses. There they had to follow the new rituals of survival.

But physical survival was not the only issue. Now they had to learn to live like white people. So many changes so quickly, coerced or not, put the survival of the Lakota *culture* in question. Indeed, by the mid-1890s, entire Lakota communities were observing the American Fourth of July holiday, with their own celebrations and dances or in conjunction with white communities. And in spite of the bitterness about their being involved in the death of Sitting Bull, Indian Police were a strong presence on every reservation. Furthermore, Lakota men were enlisting in the U.S. Army. As a matter of fact, by the winter of 1890—the same year Sitting Bull was killed—a company of Lakota soldiers attached to the Sixteenth Infantry was stationed at the Rosebud Agency. (A further irony in that situation was that men whose culture had boasted some of the finest light cavalry in the world were now foot soldiers.)

This was the future Spotted Tail and Red Cloud had seen. A revelation had come to Spotted Tail inside a prison cell at Fort Leavenworth in the late 1850s. Red Cloud had traveled to Washington several times and was awed by the sheer numbers of white people. Both men were realists. The strength of the white man was obvious in numbers. There were more of them, and they had more weapons. Consequently, and probably reluctantly, each of them realized that, sooner or later, the Lakota would have to learn to live like whites.

Wasicu se (wah-shee-chu se), "like the whites," was the phrase. Indian agents, other government officials, and missionaries who heard the translation of those words were quick to laud Spotted Tail and Red Cloud for their wisdom. They were not aware that both men meant precisely what they said. To both of them *living* like whites did not mean *becoming* white. Both were afraid that living like white people would sooner or later take from the Lakota the essence of being Lakota. And forces were already at work to that end.

By the mid-1880s, the reservation system in southern Dakota Territory (present-day South Dakota) was well established. White civilians were living on or near reservations, primarily at or near trading posts, military installations, and at Christian missions and parochial schools. Most of them were engaged in employment directly or indirectly connected to reservations or the Indian Bureau. In short, the influence of white America had already come to the reservations. And it was not going away.

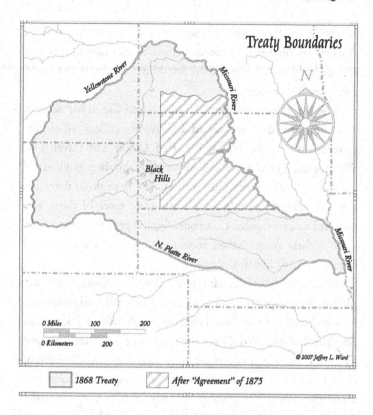

Treaty Boundaries

Yellowstone River

Missouri River

N

Black Hills

N. Platte River

Missouri River

0 Miles   100   200

0 Kilometers   200

© 2007 Jeffrey L. Ward

1868 Treaty   After "Agreement" of 1875

Kill the Indian and save the man

GOVERNMENT AND PAROCHIAL SCHOOLS were also in full swing. Those institutions were the most effective tools in the government's push for assimilation. All of them were more or less the reservation versions of the Carlisle Indian School in Pennsylvania. Carlisle's apparent success in providing a mainstream education to hundreds, if not thousands, of native children was the shining example for all such institutions to follow.

But Carlisle's success, of course, meant nothing less than confusion, humiliation, trauma, and heartache for the children who were touted as success stories. Most of them were not there of their own, or their parents', free will, and most were separated from their families and homes for years. While a few Lakota leaders and parents realized that a formal education would be necessary for their children to be able to survive and function within the new order, they could not have foreseen the hardships their children would have to endure. The cemetery for students who died while at Carlisle is mute testimony that many children, from several different tribes, were casualties of the process.

Lakota children were certainly taught the three R's, the same as Euro-American children. But before that could happen, they had to learn the English language, and that process began with an unyielding rule: The Lakota language was not to be spoken, ever again. Long hair for boys was also forbidden. Usually on the first day of school, boys sat in the barber's chair for the first lesson about their new identity: short hair. One former student recalls watching long braid after long braid tossed into a wooden box, and having the sense that lives were being tossed away.

Parochial and government boarding schools were doing their part in civilizing the Lakota. Christian denominations that did not or could not operate boarding schools nevertheless made great efforts to covert the Lakota to Christianity. This was simply a continuation of the colonialist mind-set. Missionaries had already been on the scene and as much a part of the landscape as rivers and mountains. In some instances, they led the way for other whites. But now that the so-called Indian wars were over and the Lakota were at the mercy of the U.S. government, the situation was ripe for missionaries. The missionary mind-set, however, was not exclusive to missionaries.

In 1879, Judge Elmer Dundy, of Omaha, ruled in favor of Standing Bear in *Standing Bear v. Crook*. The case was essentially about a group of Ponca Indians refusing relocation to Indian Territory. They had been duped into going there (from what is now north central Nebraska) in the first place and walked back to their home territory under the most difficult of circumstances, enduring dreadful hardships. They were taken in by the Omahas and were living with them when the government caught up with them again.

Standing Bear, the leader, asserted that he and his fellow Ponca were indeed trying to become civilized and were in the process of shedding their native identity; therefore, they should not be forcibly removed to Indian Territory. Judge Dundy agreed on exactly that basis. One sentence from his one-thousand-word opinion sums up the prevailing attitude of white America toward native peoples. Standing Bear's son had died in Oklahoma, and he and his wife wanted to reinter him in the earth of their ancestral homelands. Judge Dundy commented on that desire this way:

> Such instances of parental affection, and such love of home and native land, may be *heathen* in origin, but it seems to me they are not unlike *christian* in principle.

They were heathens, of course, in the eyes of Christians because they did not acknowledge or accept the Christian God. The indigenous peoples of North America had been labeled as such from the beginning of European contact, and the process of converting natives to Christianity had been a never-ending task. But it became a lot easier at this juncture on the northern plains because the target population was in the throes of traumatic up-heaval and was never more ripe for the picking. The missionaries waded in.

A hidden agenda

WHILE BOARDING SCHOOLS were turning the Lakota into productive citizens, and missionaries were saving their souls, the government concerned itself with their lands. Its tools were not books or Bibles, however. The U.S. government had the Dawes Act. It knew that part of the key to eradicating native culture was to control their land. But that was a secondary objective.

The Dawes Severalty Act, or General Allotment Act, of 1887 was the final mechanism that secured the procurement of Lakota lands. Its passage was not general knowledge among the Lakota. Consequently, there was little awareness that it was being implemented.

Thirty-six years earlier, while negotiating safe passage through Lakota territory as one of the provisions of the 1851 Fort Laramie Treaty, the U.S. government's peace commission-ers had assured the Lakota (and other tribes) that the emigrants would need room only for the "width of their wagons' wheels." Seventeen years after that, the 1868 treaty described the entire western half of the current state of South Dakota as the Great Sioux Reservation, where the various Lakota bands could make their homes. Attached to it was the "unceded territory" (see map, page 170), wherein the people could hunt. Seven years later, the commissioners were waiving the Agreement of 1875, which sliced off the western third of the Great Sioux Reservation, including the Black Hills and its gold. By the time most of the Lakota realized that the trend was not in their favor, the United States had further divided the remaining tract into separate reservations.

Everyone, except for those born on the agencies after the late 1860s, was painfully and angrily aware that something had been lost that probably could never be recovered. Space was not the only issue, however. The freedom to move as often and as far as they chose was limited by boundaries. The reality of the new and ever-diminishing boundaries was hardest on those who had lived the free-roaming nomadic lifestyle, especially those of the generation who could remember when a single buffalo herd covered the land from one horizon to the next.

Yet within the exterior boundaries of the various reservations, the Lakota still managed to satisfy the ancient urge to move. Families would pack their belongings in the wagons—a few still used the ancient *sungonkinpi*, the "horse carry," also called the pony drag. The French called it *travois*. Visiting relatives was as good a reason as any to pack up and move, or going to a feast or a funeral, or digging turnips. The blood of the nomad did not understand boundaries.

But even as the Lakota were grudgingly becoming accustomed to artificial boundaries on their lands and in their lives, the Dawes Act was drawing boundaries *within* each reservation, which meant more limitations and new rules. Some of those new rules meant that the Lakota would not be the only kind of people on the land.

The land was subdivided into 160- and 80-acre tracts, and then allotted. The first allotments began around 1890 and were completed by 1910. There was, of course, surplus land. That surplus land was opened for homesteading by whites. Forty-two years after the Fort Laramie Treaty promised that the Great Sioux Reservation (and the unceded lands attached to it) would belong to the Lakota in perpetuity, whites were claiming ownership by homesteading land within reservation borders.

White homesteading of reservation lands is characterized differently by two separate viewpoints. It was a breach of promise, one among many, as far as the Lakota (and other native tribes) were concerned. On the other hand, it was deemed entirely necessary by the U.S. government, which hoped that "civilization," that is, white society, would rub off on the Lakota. White homesteaders would act as role models by showing their Lakota neighbors the virtues of hard work and the proper way to use the land. Furthermore, the Lakota needed to learn that owning land in severalty was preferable to collective ownership.

Differing philosophies about the land was the flashpoint in the so-called clash of cultures. Land, as in the Earth, had always been a part of the Lakota identity, as much as brown skin, long hair, language, customs, traditions, and values, and that identity was manifested in a lifestyle that allowed them to use the resources of the land (territory) they *controlled*. Controlling a given area, however, was not the same as *owning* it. The Lakota, therefore, had not fought for ownership of land; they had fought for the freedom to live their lifestyle. But in the end, in the same way they had accepted geographic boundaries, they accepted the reality that they would own the land in the same way they owned their clothing and their dwellings.

As for "civilization" rubbing off on the Lakota, that is still in question, depending on how civilization is defined. But one fact is difficult to ignore. *White* civilization did rub off thousands and thousands of acres of Lakota lands.

The authors of the Dawes Act could not have conceived a better long-range plan to ensure that every acre of Indian land would one day be acquired, one way or another, by whites. White homesteading of surplus lands after allotment was only the first step.

It is important to note that the Choctaw and Cherokee down in the Indian Territory of Oklahoma refused allotment, and dared to take their case to federal court. The U.S. Congress promptly passed the Curtis Act, specifically aimed at them, dissolving their tribal governments and forcing allotment on them.

The federal government was confident that the Lakota, the epitome of prereservation nomadic hunters of the plains, would turn to tilling the land, making appropriate use of it, as it were. That did not happen, of course. So Congress changed the rules again and passed legislation allowing whites to lease individually owned Lakota lands. Of course, the lease transaction was not conducted directly between the lessee—the white farmer—and the lessor—the Lakota land owner. The Bureau of Indian Affairs, as trustee for the United States of America, leased the land for the landowner. Many transactions occurred either without the knowledge or consent of the landowner.

Even from the perspective of the current moment, it is difficult to decide whether white America wanted native lands more than they wanted to eradicate native cultures. At some point, however, came the realization that taking the land was the same as eradicating the cultures that had lived on it and with it. Nevertheless, Europeans and Euro-Americans had coveted the land from the beginning.

Land was acquired by negotiation (which is another word for

trickery, some natives say), by force, or by legislation. However it was taken, the people who lost their lands also stood in danger of losing their cultures. The 1868 Fort Laramie Treaty not only established boundaries, but also inducements for the Lakota to adopt the Euro-American lifestyle. For example,

- Under Article 4, the United States agreed, at its own expense, to build warehouses, agency buildings, a physician's residence, and buildings for carpenters, farmers, blacksmiths, millers, and engineers. A schoolhouse or a mission building would be built if enough children could be induced to attend school.
- Article 6 offered an individual allotment not to exceed 320 acres for any head of family who decided to be a farmer.
- Article 8 stated that if the agent saw that the head of the family really intended to farm, he would receive seeds and agricultural implements, paid for by the government, of course, and possibly up to three years more. Furthermore, the government would teach him how to farm.
- Article 14 offered an outright reward of five hundred dollars for up to ten people who grew the most valuable crops each year for three years running.

Allotment took direct aim at Lakota identity as well. Once a man signed to accept his 160 acres, he was more or less forced to perform a strange ceremony. He was given a bow and one arrow and taken to a single bottom plow. He was then instructed to shoot the arrow into the distance, throw down the bow, and grab the handles of the plow. The symbolism of casting aside the bow for the plow was obvious. He was casting aside his old identity for a new one. The hunter/warrior was now to be a farmer.

But there was more than symbolism to the Dawes Severalty Act. Theodore Roosevelt succinctly summed up the true sentiment of Congress when he said the act was a "vast pulverizing engine to break up the tribal mass." Congress intended the transition of native lands from communal ownership to individual ownership to compel natives to become fully participating members of American society, to the detriment of their own. That consequence was exactly what Congress had in mind. The needs of the community would become secondary to the needs of the individual. The authors of the Dawes Act assumed that natives were discontent with the condition of their lives and therefore would embrace any system or method enabling them to improve their lot. They could not understand that natives, by and large, were more discontent with the way the U.S. government, and whites in general, were treating them. That compelled them to band together tighter as families and communities, instead of "bettering" themselves individually. The tribal masses stayed together. Their land holdings were another story.

It is difficult to deny that the Dawes Severalty/General Allotment/Homestead Act was created expressly as a mechanism to diminish native land holdings. Over the course of its life, the Dawes Act contributed to the loss of millions of acres. In 1902, Congress allowed natives to sell inherited lands, and in 1906, the Burke Act lifted restrictions and enabled individuals to sell their allotments. The Wheeler-Howard Act, or Indian Reorganization Act of 1934, generally reversed the Dawes Act and allowed tribes as well as individuals to own land. But the damage had been done. White ranchers, farmers, and speculators learned how to circumvent the system to obtain cheap land. The trusteeship status of the Bureau of Indian Affairs was to have safeguarded the interests of individual natives and tribes. But the complicity, if not outright corruption, of officials at the agency level made a mockery of the Bureau's role as an advocate.

Furthermore, the Dawes Act continues to achieve its true purpose. In 1977, the Supreme Court of the United States reduced the exterior boundaries of the Rosebud Sioux Tribe of South Dakota. The tribe attempted to circumvent the state's move to redraw the boundaries in *Rosebud Sioux Tribe v. Kneip*, but it lost at every level of the federal court system. In the end, the Supreme Court agreed with the state's contention that four of the five counties within the original exterior borders were no longer part of the reservation. That position was based on the fact that non-Lakota people owned more land within those counties than the tribe or individual tribal members combined. The percentage was approximately 60 percent non-Indian ownership to 40 percent Indian.

The loss of that land base began when the first white homesteader squatted on his 160 acres, under the provisions of the Dawes Act, and saw possibilities.

SIXTEEN

New Ways, New Words

SHORTLY AFTER the turn of the nineteenth century, a Lakota man was about to go to the agency trading post for a few supplies. His wife asked him to buy her some shoes. "*Hanpa iyeyapi etan makaku ye,*" she instructed. On his way home from the trading post, the man went by the local dump and found a pair of women's shoes that had been discarded. Needless to say, his wife was not happy when he gave her someone else's castoffs. "But," he defended himself, "I did exactly what you asked me to do." Indeed, he had.

The man's wife had said, "Bring me home some found shoes." The key word was *iyeyapi*, which means "something found." But the man had forgotten that the word had also come to mean "to lace." High, laced ankle shoes were the style for women's shoes at the time. His wife had meant, "Bring me home some lace-up shoes." The man, of course, made up for his mistake and bought his wife new lace-up shoes. And he probably never forget the other meaning for *iyeyapi*.

Languages can and do reflect the changes societies undergo. Languages evolve over time under normal circumstances (if there is such a thing as normal circumstances). When the change is rapid or traumatic, however, new words and phrases often tell their own story of impact and change.

In the late 1600s, the Lakota were forced out of the lake region of what is now Minnesota. The instrument of change then was the firearm. The Anishinabe people acquired muzzle-loading rifles from the French in sufficient numbers to tip the balance of military power in their favor and drive out the Lakota. A new phrase, *maza wakan* (mah-zah wah-khan), was born out of that pivotal time. *Maza* meant "metal" or "iron." *Wakan* had several different connotations, such as "holy," "sacred," "mysterious," or "difficult to understand." Although the materials that went into the construction of the "holy iron" were obvious—iron and wood—the precise manner in which the weapon functioned was initially a mystery. Consequently, the first and most common translation into English for firearm was "holy iron."

Lost in the obvious notoriety of "holy iron," however, is another, definitely more descriptive meaning: *ioksupi* (ee-oh-kshoo-be), or "loaded by the mouth." As any gun aficionado knows, powder and shot for the rifles and handguns of that era were loaded down the muzzle, which is the mouth of the gun.

"Loaded by the mouth" certainly doesn't have the mystery or romance of "holy iron." Therefore, *maza wakan* was the phrase used most often because it was more generic, especially because the firearm changed as time went on. The *ioksupi*, or muzzle-loader, was replaced by the breechloader, described as *lazatan oksupi* (lah-zah-tan oh-kshoo-be), or "loaded from the back or rear." That gave way to the repeating rifle, which was simply *ota oksupi* (oh-tah oh-kshoo-be), or "loaded many times," or *ota kutepi* (oh-tah koo-deh-be), or "fired many times." The pistol was simply *isakpe* (ee-shah-kpeh), or "six mouths," meaning, of course, the six rounds in the chambers.

Other accoutrements introduced by Europeans and Euro-Americans to the Lakota were eyeglasses, photographs, liquor, clocks, schoolhouses, books, churches, hospitals, automobiles, and airplanes, among many others.

Ista maza (ee-shtah mah-zah), two words meaning "eye or eyes" and "iron" became eyeglasses. The phrase literally means "iron eyes." The descriptor for eyeglasses is because the first eyeglasses seen by our ancestors were made from metal and glass.

Wicitowapi (wee-chee-do-wah-be) was used to describe a photograph, from two words *wiciti* (wee-chee-teh), meaning "face or human face," and *owapi* (oh-wah-be), meaning "to sketch or draw."

While eyeglasses were a totally new object for the Lakota, the idea of sketching or drawing a face was not too far removed from a photograph. The process involved was more of a mystery than the firearm, especially because very few Euro-Americans had a precise enough command of the Lakota language to explain how a camera worked. Therefore, a certain amount of mystery surrounded photographs for several decades. But not all new objects, materials, or ideas were that innocuous.

Liquor was not common among the Lakota or many other native peoples. In fact, it was another one of those words that had to be coined to describe what it was. Most contemporary native Lakota speakers, when asked to translate the adjective *drunk* (inebriated) would say *itomni* (ee-doh-mnee). The word also and originally meant "dizzy." Although there is not one common term for liquor, there are words for the different types: *Mnisa* (mnee-shah), literally meaning "red water," was and is the word for *wine*; *mnipiga* (mnee-be-gah), literally "boiling water," was and is the word for *beer*. "Boiling water" did not mean that beer was boiled, but it described the fizzy carbonation effect.

There are, however, other more difficult factors relative to alcohol. *Wayatkanpi* (wah-yah-tkanh-be) means "to drink" or "they drink" in reference to someone who drinks heavily or is an alcoholic. Alcoholism is the second most serious health problem for Lakota people and natives overall. (The most serious is diabetes.) An unfortunate and denigrating myth is that all natives are drunkards, or alcoholics, which is simply not the case. But alcohol has been a serious social problem since the very first time it was introduced to the northern plains.

Crazy Horse saw firsthand the effects of alcohol. When he was young, an elderly acquaintance of his was shot and killed by a man under the influence. Consequently, Crazy Horse detested alcohol and anyone who had anything to do with it. Ironically, within the past ten years, a brewing company—either from sheer arrogance or surprising ignorance—marketed a malt liquor using the Crazy Horse name. The company had the good sense to change the name after considerable uproar from the Lakota community.

It would be remiss not to mention that each and every Lakota, Dakota, and Nakota tribe has programs to help people recover from alcohol (and drug) dependency. Many of the programs incorporate traditional spiritual beliefs into the treatment programs, and they have achieved significant success.

Indian time

BEFORE THE WHITE MAN CAME, the Lakota had no word for time. There were words for sunrise, dawn, morning, noon, sunset, evening, dusk, night, tomorrow, yesterday, past, and future. Lakota lifestyle did not require a structure for a concept that basically did not exist. If someone said, "I will come to your lodge in the morning," that meant he or she had from sunrise to noon to arrive, and that was good enough. If one wanted to be more precise, he or she would say, "I will come to your lodge at sunset." Either way, the obligation was not to a time but simply to an arrival. That inherent, cultural nonallegiance to time was a source of frustration to Euro-Americans. But in time (no pun intended), the Lakota adjusted, somewhat, to the way time was structured. And it began with an object, and not the concept.

Mazaskanskan (mah-zah-shkan-shkan) became the word for *clock*. Literally it meant "iron that moves" or "moving iron," referring to the hands of the clock. *Oape* (oh-ah-peh), meaning to "strike within," became the word for *hour*, which described early clocks chiming or striking on the hour. *Oape cika* (oh-ah-peh gee-kah), which is rather nonsensical when taken literally (a small striking within), colloquially meant "little hour," or "minute."

Since the Lakota did not worry about measuring or delineating time, being on time or keeping an appointment did not mean the same as it did to whites. Hence the derogatory phrase "Indian time" was coined. But the Lakota and overall native attitude about time lives on. They do understand the European and Euro-American obsession with the measurement of time, and they will live by and with it, for the most part. But they also believe that starting and completing a task or an event at a given minute or hour is not quite as important as just doing it. Whenever.

Counting and reading

WHILE MEASURING TIME was not a requirement in prereservation Lakota society, there was an educational process. But that process was not separate from the family or community, and there was not a separate place where children were taught. The educational process was a one-on-one mentoring system. The women of the family taught girls the skills to care for home and family. They explained childbearing and child rearing and the sacred calling of the woman to be the focal point of family. Likewise, men taught boys to be providers and protectors. But as white people and their lifestyle and attitudes became more and more a part of Lakota life, the Lakota soon learned that there was a new and strange approach to teaching children. And the Lakota found ways to describe that new strangeness.

Owayawa (oh-wah-yah-wah) means "to count inside" (meaning a structure), and that became the word for *school*. A school was a building where Lakota children were taken into and made to count: *yawa*. Eventually, *yawa* came to mean "to read."

Wowapi (woe-wah-be) described the *book*, but it is literally "to mark or to write." It is based on the word *owa* (oh-wah), which means "to mark," and that logically also came to mean "write." *Wowapi yawa* literally means "to count the marks," but it also means "to read a book."

Where does God live?

CHURCHES WERE PART of parochial boarding schools. Spirituality was not unknown to the Lakota, and there were religious ceremonies as old (and probably older) than Christianity. But again, the different way in which Christianity approached religion was reflected in Lakota words.

Owacekiye (oh-wah-cheh-kee-yeh) meant "a place to pray," and that described a *church*. *Tipi wakan* (tee-be wah-khan), or "holy dwelling," was also a phrase for *church*. It was a specifically designated place in which to pray, somewhat implying that it was the only place one could pray. Prayer was part of the everyday life of the Lakota long before the arrival of Christianity, and prayers could be said or offered anywhere. The idea that God lived only in a certain place or could be approached only from a specific location was foreign to Lakota people. To them, God lives in all things and hears our prayers from anywhere they are prayed.

Like the Euro-American approach to education and religion, the practice of healing the sick or injured also seemed, to the Lakota, somewhat segregated from the community. That assessment was reflected in how the Lakota described a hospital.

To fix or repair

HOSPITAL has a very interesting translation in Lakota. *Okujetipi* is a combination of a preposition, an adjective, and a noun. *Okuje* (oh-koo-jeh) combines *o*, the preposition *in*, and *kuje*, the adjective *ill*. Therefore, *okuje* is "ill in" or "to be ill in," and *tipi* is the noun that means "dwelling," "house," or "building." The translation for *hospital* is a "place to be ill in." The name indicates the reluctance that many Lakota had to going to a hospital. It obviously was not a place of healing; it was a place to go and become ill. Furthermore, the Lakota word for *hospital* is somewhat of a statement concerning their opinion of Euro-American medical practices.

Doctors were part of the early reservations, of course. By and large, however, doctors and priests looked down on native healers, known as medicine men. The Lakota called them *wapiya wicasa* (wah-pee-yah wee-chah-shah), which meant "the man who repairs or heals." They were also know as *wicasa wakan* (wee-chah-shah wah-khan), or "holy man." These labels indicate that the Lakota understood that a healer or medicine man had powers and abilities that other people did not. Many of them, for example, knew about medicinal plants and how to use them. If spiritual beliefs and religious practices were considered heathen, the healing practices of medicine men were considered primitive (at the very least) and ineffectual. It should be noted that in the *Lakota-English Dictionary*, by Eugene Buechel, S.J., the definition for *wapiya* (to repair, to heal) is "to conjure the sick." The apparent editing of a Lakota word by a non-Lakota linguist (and Jesuit priest) is indicative of the attitudes of priests and physicians toward medicine men. Doctors and priests discredited medicine men at every opportunity. Their complaints against medicine men often resulted in arrests by Indian police. Over time, as more and more Lakota people availed themselves of the services offered by white doctors, they began to call them *wicasa wakan*.

Speaking white

SOME WORDS that necessarily evolved from Lakota and white interaction reflected how the Lakota looked at themselves. One of the most discussed and debated words among Lakota speakers is *iyeska* (ee-yeh-skah), meaning "speaks white." An *iyeska* was anyone who spoke English. But more than that, initially, an *iyeska* was usually a white male (although a few black men also fell into the category) who, from close contact with Lakota people, had learned the Lakota language and could act as an interpreter. But it could also describe a Lakota who had learned to speak English. Therefore the word basically describes a language skill or ability.

Iyeska, however, attained a somewhat derogatory connotation when it was used to mean someone of mixed racial parentage, or a "mixed-blood." That label was used by those who were, or considered themselves to be, pure or "full-blood" Lakota to describe anyone who had any amount of white blood. Full-bloods considered themselves to be more traditional Lakota than mixed-bloods, who were thought to be more white in their thinking or values because of their white blood. It is, all in all, a very divisive debate. Fortunately, most Lakota know that cultural foundation comes from the knowledge and values of a family's influence, regardless of the extent of Lakota or white blood.

Chairs, shoes, and calendars

SOME EXISTING Lakota words took on a slightly different meaning. The two best examples are *oakanke* and *hanpa*. *Oakanke* (oh-ah-khan-keh) means "chair," or "to sit on." It is now more frequently translated as *backrest*, which describes the only chair the Lakota used: the lattice of willow rods attached to a tripod of stout poles. This piece of furniture stood on the floor, and the user sat on it on the floor. When the European four-legged chair arrived on the scene, *oakanke* was used to describe it. Over time, someone made a differentiation between the willow chair and the four-legged chair, calling the willow chair a backrest.

Hanpa (han-bah) or *moccasin* was subject to the same demotion, if you will. After European shoes came onto the scene, *hanpa* became the word for *shoe*. *Hanpa ikceya* (han-bah ee-kceh-yah) became the phrase for *moccasin*, and it meant "common or lesser shoe," implying, of course, that the moccasin was inferior.

Another aspect of our culture that changed to fit the new

Euro-American order was our thirteen-month calendar based on the cycles of the moon. A month was twenty-six to twenty-nine days, and the name for each month was descriptive of a significant environmental event or consequence. For example, the third month of the year was known as *Istawicayazanpi Wi* (ee-shtah-wee-chah-yah-zan-be wee), or Month When Eyes Are Hurting, also known as the Month of Snow Blindness.

A *wiyawapi* should not, however, be confused with *waniyetu yawapi* (wah-knee-yeh-due yah-wah-be), which is "counting the winters" or "they count the winters." The more well-known term is *winter count*. A winter count was a family or community record, a combination of pictures and information committed to memory. At least one picture was drawn by the keeper of the winter count to represent the most significant event of the year, and the keeper could vividly describe that event and the reason it was chosen as the most significant. From that he could also recall other events that occurred within that given year.

Waniyetu is "winter," and it was used as the marker for the passage of an entire year because winter was the toughest season of the year. It was a matter of some distinction for an elder to say "Waniyetu masakowin," or "I am seventy winters," because it also meant that he or she had survived that many winters.

Wiyawapi and *waniyetu yawapi* are intrinsic parts of our culture. But the next word is not.

Of the people

AMONG MANY NATIVE TRIBES the common name usually was some form of "the people." Our names are based on something different.

As mentioned in chapter 4, the three parts of the overall nation of people are Dakota, Nakota, and Lakota. Each word is a different dialect of the parent language and means "friends" or "alliance of friends." Variations of the word preceded each and were the basis for those names because of their meanings.

Olakolkiciyapi (oh-lah-khol-kee-chee-yah-be) means "to treat one another as friends" and "to make peace with one another."

Olakowicaya (oh-lah-khol-wee-chah-yah) means "to care about."

Olakol (oh-lah-khol) and *olakota* (oh-lah-kho-dah) both mean "to make friends" or "to make peace among." Later it was applied to the treaty-making process with whites.

Olakolya (oh-lah-khol-yah) means "to have for a friend." *Kola* (khoh-lah), which means "friend," comes from this word.

In the early 1970s, an elder named Isaac Bear Shield stood to address the Rosebud Sioux Tribal Council. He spoke in Lakota, of course.

"Winter is coming," he said. "The children are crying because they are cold and hungry. They are looking to you to keep them warm and feed them."

Mr. Bear Shield was a traditionalist, and he was the very first tribal president at Rosebud after the implementation of the 1934 Wheeler-Howard Act. The literal message he delivered was necessary, but the figurative one was just as important. He was directly reminding the members of the tribal council of their duty to the people. He concluded his speech with the following words:

"*Wolakota ogna skanpo*" (wo-lah-khoh-dah oh-gahna shkan-bo).

The phrase has several interpretations, but the message Mr. Bear Shield wanted the tribal council members to hear was simple and ancient: "Do this in the Lakota way."

We are fortunate as Lakota that the essence of our culture has survived. We are one of only half a dozen indigenous nations where at least 30 per cent of the population speak their native language. We accept the fact that assimilation has changed us, but we also know that it did not re-create us. That part, we are doing ourselves. And we will take our customs, traditions, values, and our language, as well as the ancient and modern versions of ourselves, into the twenty-first century and beyond.

Furthermore, we will continue to do this in the Lakota way.

SEVENTEEN

The "Conqueror's" Mentality

IN 1923, A DIRECTIVE was sent by Charles Burke, Commissioner of the Bureau of Indian Affairs, to Superintendents of the Bureau in the field. It was labeled Indian Dancing: Supplement to Circular No. 1665. Commissioner Burke caused to be written several recommendations enacted at a conference of Christian ministers working among the Lakota.

The directive was really a set of restrictions, promulgated in the "best welfare" of the various tribes now under the control of the government. The restrictions specified

- That the Indian form of gambling and lottery known as the *ituranpi*, "give away," be prohibited.
- That the Indian dances be limited to one each month in the daylight hours of one day in the midweek, and at one center in each district; the months of March and April, June, July, and August excepted.
- That none take part in the dances, or be present who are under 50 years of age.
- That a careful propaganda be undertaken to educate public opinion against the dance and to provide a healthy substitute.

The mentality of the "conqueror" was paternalistic from the very beginning. Two hundred years ago Lewis and Clark were announcing the president of the United States as the "Great Father" to the native tribes they encountered. Commissioner Burke did not deviate from this attitude, and it was one that was omnipresent on Lakota reservations.

After Wounded Knee, the Lakota faced the reality of their situation and tried to make the best of it. To some, survival in itself was a victory of the spirit. To most others, though, living in the new order was a bitter pill to swallow. But swallow it they did as they moved on, including the many who refused to forget who they were and where they had come from.

More than a few Lakota people rationalized that their world had ended at the Little Bighorn. There were some who even said that their victory motivated the whites to act more swiftly to put the Lakota on reservations. The nation of the Long Knives wanted nothing less than to get the Lakota out of the way in order to possess more land.

But getting the Lakota out of the way of a growing nation did not mean leaving them to their own means. There were a few years free of intrusive interference from the Bureau of Indian Affairs (BIA) when horses and wagons enabled families to move within the confines of the reservation, but making a living was not easy. Some Lakota turned to growing crops, not because the U.S. government wanted them to farm, but because families had to be fed. At first it was the women who planted small plots of corn and beans because they were easy to air dry, which was the age-old method of preserving food. It was also a way to augment the issued beef—Texas longhorns mostly—the main source of meat. But it was a poor substitute for buffalo.

Life was different for the forty and above age group, those that could remember life before the Battle of the Little Bighorn era. Little by little, there were fewer and fewer soldiers. Most of the men in blue uniforms were Lakota recruited to be policemen. Some Lakota would venture to say that life now was as good as it could be, under the circumstances. And even during those few years of quiet, things happening behind closed doors half a continent away continued to control Lakota life. Life may have been as good as it could be under the circumstances, but some of those circumstances were downright disheartening.

That subtle psychological affront was reinforced when the people were forbidden to observe the Sun Dance. Missionaries viewed the dance as an obstacle to converting the Lakota to Christianity, and they wanted it stopped. The government obliged. The circle of the sweat lodge, used in the *inipi* ceremony, was under attack also. Priests and pastors complained to Indian Agents, who sent Indian police to find and destroy sweat lodges. Consequently, many Lakota went straight from the circle of the Sun Dance and sweat lodge into square churches.

So perhaps the assessment that life was as good as it could be under the circumstances was correct. Fortunately, the people no longer had to defend themselves militarily, but it was now just as necessary to defend themselves in other ways. Though many Lakota did embrace Christianity, there were a few who stubbornly clung to the spiritual beliefs and practices they had followed all of their lives. In order to contend with and understand the thinking of the people who styled themselves as their "conquerors," they called on their ability to adapt, and entire generations of Lakota learned to speak English. They also wanted somehow to circumvent the impact of boarding schools on their children and grandchildren. If the Lakota language was taken from the younger generations, parents and grandparents wanted to at least hand down their culture in English. There were no longer any military conflicts, but there were difficulties of every other kind.

The mind-set of the "conqueror" could not have been manifested more insidiously, or more secretively, than at a small community beyond the borders of the Lakota reservations. An institution, the brainchild of white politicians, began its life even as the Lakota were beginning to come to grips with life on a reservation. During its thirty-three years of existence, the Canton Asylum for Insane Indians was the epitome of paternalism and self-righteousness.

South Dakota had been a state for nearly nine years when Senator Richard F. Pettigrew testified before his Senate colleagues in 1898 regarding insane Indians. His views are succinctly expressed in the following excerpt.

It has been well established that the percentage of insanity is greater among half-breeds than among full-blooded Indians. That is explained by the theory of crossbreeding, that has a tendency to weaken the race. For this reason it is confidently expected by those who have made a study of these conditions, that the rate of insanity will greatly increase as our civilization develops. The peculiar mental affliction of the Indians make it impractical to treat them in connection with white patients. Association with their ancient enemy has, it is said, a harrowing effect upon them. Also it has been

demonstrated by experience that the various State Asylums
for the treatment of the insane are not kindly disposed to re-
ceiving Indian patients.

It was a two-pronged attack. Congressman Oscar Gifford
testified in the House of Representatives, with the following
words of wisdom:

> The necessity for an asylum for the treatment of insane In-
> dians has become a special interest to the people of South
> Dakota because of their proximity to the Reservations of all
> the Western States. The value of favorable surrounding rec-
> ognized in the treatment of insane whites, has been entirely
> ignored in the case of the Redskin, with their insane growing
> more neglected, violent, and unmanageable. We are asking
> for the means to apply on the same basis the treatment for
> the Indian people that is applied to his white brother.

In 1899, the U.S. Congress authorized the establishment of
the Canton Asylum for Insane Indians, to be built near the small
town of Canton, in eastern South Dakota. Later it came to be
known as the Hiawatha Asylum. An initial appropriation of
forty-five thousand dollars was for construction of the facility
and the purchase of one hundred acres. The land purchase was
arranged by Congressman Oscar Gifford, a former mayor of
Canton. After construction was completed in 1902, Gifford became the asylum's first superintendent. On December 31 of that
year the first patient was admitted. He died several months later
during an epileptic seizure.

The Canton Asylum was the administrative and operational

responsibility of the Bureau of Indian Affairs, and for obvious reasons. The BIA had jurisdiction over the "half-breeds," whose rate of insanity was apparently growing by leaps and bounds, and becoming more "violent and unmanageable" as well. These goings-on were, of course, not common knowledge on the reservations in South Dakota, but they were something of an economic boon to the Canton area. Every year, for thirty-three years, the asylum received tens of thousands of dollars in funding.

Superintendent Gifford was forced to resign in 1908 amid rumors and complaints of patient neglect and abuse. He was replaced by Dr. Harry Hummer, a psychiatrist who had been on the staff at St. Elizabeth's Hospital in Washington, D.C. Several employees later charged that Dr. Hummer also mistreated patients. A federal investigator was called in, and he concluded that Hummer "is ill-tempered but doing an adequate job."

Reports of patient abuse and mistreatment continued to leak out, including rapes of female inmates. One of several subsequent investigations stated that most of the patients were not mentally ill. Many of them, however, were considered troublemakers by the BIA, such as medicine men, people who resisted reservation life, or students who could not or would not fit into boarding schools, and so on. Many were sent to the asylum on orders from the BIA because the institution needed patients.

In 1916, a hospital was added and the asylum's capacity increased to eighty-five patients. In 1925, BIA commissioner Charles Burke inspected the facility and reported seeing a man chained to his bed, and only one attendant supervising ninety patients. He then authorized Dr. Hummer to hire more attendants and purchase more modern patient restraints. In 1928, Congress appropriated funds to expand the asylum.

The capacity of the asylum was about ninety patients, with approximately half of them women. Only a few were ever declared "cured" and allowed to go home. Patients were brought to the asylum from several different reservations throughout the west. But a significant number were from the South Dakota and North Dakota reservations. Many were Lakota.

In 1929, a psychiatrist, Dr. Samuel Silk, investigated the asylum at the request of the federal government. His report read, in part:

> Three patients were found padlocked in rooms. One was sick in bed, supposed to be suffering from a brain tumor, being bedridden and helpless . . . a boy about 10 years of age was in a strait jacket lying in his bed . . . one patient who had been in the hospital six years was padlocked in a room and, according to the attendant, had been secluded in this room for nearly three years.

Dr. Silk concluded that the asylum's patients received the poorest medical care. Consequently, Secretary of the Interior Ray Wilbur ordered Dr. Hummer's removal, but Congressman Louis Cramton of South Dakota intervened, and the battle over the asylum began.

In 1933, the new commissioner of the BIA, John Collier, ordered the asylum closed. The opposition from the South Dakota congressional delegation was fierce and predictable. They argued vehemently that the town of Canton would suffer extreme economic hardship. Dr. Hummer would later be dismissed by no less than the Secretary of the Interior, Harold Ickes. In a last ditch effort to save the asylum, its supporters approached Lakota leaders on the reservations, asking for their help to keep it open. Their audacious assertion was that it was better for the patients to be treated close to home, rather than in some institution hundreds of miles from home. This was the first time many Lakota people learned of the existence of the asylum.

In December of 1933, fifteen of the patients were sent home to their reservations. Sixty-nine were transferred to St. Elizabeth's Hospital in Washington, D.C. Their fates are unknown to this day, except perhaps to their descendants. The institution frequently and proudly billed by the citizens of Canton as "the world's only Indian insane asylum" was finally closed. But not before compiling a tragic record.

From 1902 to 1933, 374 Indians from sixty different tribes were listed as patients, of whom 121 died there. Their individually unmarked graves still remain, located now between the fifth and sixth fairways of the Hiawatha Golf Course. In 1946, the federal government sold the land and buildings to the City of Canton for one dollar. Though a wooden fence now surrounds the 121 graves, it cannot protect them from the frequent errant ball that lands inside. Some golfers take the free drop, which is the rule for the course. Others still play their ball where it lies, often from atop a grave. The mentality of the "conqueror" remains alive and well.

In the midst of the Canton Asylum's existence, World War I occurred. Interestingly, several of the patients sent to the institution were shell-shocked native veterans who had served in Europe. In fact, approximately eight thousand native men served during the First World War. Many would later remark that they had fought as mercenaries for the United States of America. They were technically correct, since none of them were citizens at the time. That would change.

The U.S. Congress passed the Indian Citizenship Act in 1924, grandiosely declaring it was the nation's appreciation for the military service of natives during the First World War. As it turned out, Congress did not put the question of citizenship before the various tribes before it enacted the legislation. If it had, many of them would have debated the issue long and hard before rendering a decision. Among the Lakota, there were still many who had lived through the post–Little Bighorn era and they had vivid memories of Wounded Knee—memories that stirred deep mistrust of the U.S. government and of white society. And other tribes had their compelling reasons for not trusting the United States, so it is safe to say that some, if not many, of the tribes would have rejected U.S. citizenship.

In any case, just as the homestead provisions in the 1887 Dawes Severalty Act eroded the Lakota land base, the Citizenship Act has weakened the sovereignty of tribal nations. But even as the legal status of the Lakota (and other tribes) was placed on shaky ground, another aspect of our ancient traditions was weakened by the passage of yet another act in 1934.

This time, wisdom itself was under attack.

In 1934, came the Wheeler-Howard Act, or Indian Reorganization Act (IRA). It was a double-edged sword. On one hand, it ended the allotment of land to Indians. On the other hand, it did nothing to circumvent the loss of land to homesteaders. By then, white homesteaders had taken root on all the reservations. The moral path would have been to end and repeal the homestead provisions, pay the homesteaders fair market value for their land, and arrange an escort to the reservation boundary. On the seemingly appropriate side, the act gave native tribes the right to own land collectively and provided for self-government.

The commissioner of the BIA, John Collier, was the chief proponent of Indian Reorganization, and he probably had the best interests of Indians at heart. However, he could not have been aware that his good intentions regarding tribal "self-government" effectively undermined, over time, an age-old Lakota resource: the wisdom of elders.

In the prereservation era, the wisdom of elders was a critical guiding influence in Lakota life, whether it was sought within the family fold or by the community as a whole. Every village or community had a council of elderly men, often referred to as *wica omniciye*, or a "gathering of complete men," meaning that each man had accomplished much and had acquired wisdom; individually, the men on the council were called *woglaka wicasa*, or the "man who speaks," meaning that they spoke for all the people. Their gatherings were mostly informal, but nonetheless there existed a strict code for how meetings were conducted.

By 1934, the function of the *wica omniciye* had all but faded as a consistent factor in Lakota life, and it was on its way to becoming as much a part of the past as the bison were. So when the Wheeler-Howard Act was explained to the Lakota, it received mixed reactions and skepticism, because it would certainly speed the demise of the *wica omniciye*.

The Wheeler-Howard Act not only provided tribes with the opportunity to govern themselves, but it also provided a model: a government based on a constitution (also provided) with executive, legislative, and judicial branches. White society was still trying to recreate the Lakota in its own image. Most tribes took advantage of the Wheeler-Howard opportunity with a wait-and-see attitude. At the very least, there was the appearance of self-government, and many Lakota saw that as a good first step. But when tribal governments finally began to function, it was obvious that the game was being played according to someone else's rules. A few tribes rejected Wheeler-Howard outright and formed their own governments on a different model, but for most tribes, there were few other options.

However it came about, self-government by someone else's rules was necessary if the Lakota were to have any meaningful control over their lives and have any influence on their children's and grandchildren's future. They hoped that in time they would be able to mold that government to fit their customs, traditions, and values. As one old horse trainer advised: "To influence a wild horse, a man has to ride it in the direction it was going in the first place." So the Lakota jumped on.

In retrospect, the first generation of Lakota on the reservation had to take advantage of the only game in town, but in many ways it is still a work in progress. When the first elected tribal councils began to function, most members were older and mature men with life experiences to draw upon. But as the years went by, younger and younger men stood for election and won seats on the councils. Wisdom, the way in which it had been applied in the prereservation days, was becoming less of a factor.

In prereservation days, politics were never the most important factor, because the inherent right of individual free choice was an effective system of checks and balances. A leader was selected by the community based on common sense, but that leader—aware of the power of individual choice—was careful not to overstep his boundaries because he knew that the people could stop following him as easily as they had chosen him. But that changed with the implementation of Wheeler-Howard and the adaptation of Euro-American politics, and the inception of elected tribal councils.

With the IRA councils, the qualifications to stand for election were a minimum age, usually twenty-five, and residence within the district or community. Later a record absent of felonies became a qualification as well.

Tribes virtually had no choice. If they did not form governments under the auspices of Wheeler-Howard, or something similar, the federal government could apply pressure until tribes complied. If they did not, the BIA simply maintained control, although the BIA never really relinquished control—even after the inception of IRA councils.

In prereservation times, the members of a village council, of even a small village, had hundreds of years of combined experience. In the first shaky years of IRA councils, older men were selected, but that was not to be the trend. Long gone were the days when men were selected to lead based on their achievements and character. Early years on the reservations, prior to 1900, opened the door for a new way to rise to leadership: currying favor with the Indian agent. In that new process, skillful politicians had the advantage; those who could understand English had a higher advantage, but not as good as those who could understand as well as speak the language of the "conqueror." In short, the Lakota rolled with the flow.

There were exceptions, of course, Sitting Bull among them. He was the leader recognized by his people, the Hunkpapa Lakota, without an "appointment" by the Indian bureau as "paper chief." He was not popular with the Standing Rock agent because he disdained contact with government officials. There should have been more Sitting Bulls.

Rolling with the flow again after 1934 meant that politics, rather than common sense and achievement, got people elected to tribal councils. A young man, who met the minimum age requirement and was elected, had an equal voice with a fellow council member twice his age. In a perfect world, wisdom rises to the top, but to some younger men, sitting on a tribal council was a heady experience. And then, as now, staying on the council became a priority. Therefore, no matter how often or how eloquently the voices of wisdom spoke, there were enough younger men who learned the game of politics and did not hesitate to add their voices to the din. In that din the voices of wisdom were lost. The flow of a new age weakened them considerably.

Over the years there has been debate about the legal impacts and ramifications of any number of Congressional acts like Wheeler-Howard. Books have been written pro and con on the social and legal consequences of that act and other legislation. Native and nonnative scholars have waded in on whatever issue or topic they have chosen to expound on. Yet there is very little on the *cultural* impact of the Dawes Severalty Act, the Indian Citizenship Act, or the Wheeler-Howard Act. Since the BIA is not likely to convene a conference on the cultural impact of Congressional legislation, it is critical that native peoples and groups find ways to do so themselves. One of the first and continuing topics of discussion should be the wisdom of elders. Theirs are the voices that should be heard, and theirs are the insights that should be sought, whether they sit on any council or not.

The Lakota still must face important issues: land and sovereignty, housing, education, health care, and gaming, to name some. Without a doubt, they are important issues that must continue to remain the focus of awareness of all native peoples if they are to survive.

There will be those, both native and white, who will argue

that the good old days are long gone. The Lakota no longer live in tipis and no longer hunt buffalo, and the current system of tribal government is in tune with the times. Perhaps the implication is that since the Lakota have experienced external changes, they should change internally as well. In other words, they should forget where they came from—the past. But an essential part of the past was the wisdom of elders.

Too much has already been forgotten. The necessity of wisdom should not be in that category. If the Lakota roll with the flow, as it were, and forget where they came from in the process, many feel that it would be an insult to their ancestors. It would be forgetting what those ancestors had to do in order to survive as culturally intact as possible and to pass on what had survived to the next generation. And it is the sacred duty of each generation to do the same.

Those who are Lakota culturally, no matter the thickness or thinness of ancestral blood, do understand the value of wisdom. Many were raised by an extended family where grandparents were the epitome of all the values they taught. More important, those grandparents were wise. They had earned that wisdom by living and enduring, and it is still the deepest resource the modern Lakota have to draw on. Therefore, in spite of the fact that Lakota people do not live in tipis anymore or hunt buffalo from the back of a horse—and perhaps because of those realities— they should not allow someone else's rules or will to deny that invaluable resource.

Furthermore, they should not deny it to themselves.

EIGHTEEN

The Twentieth Century

Fighting Indian fighters

A PARTICULAR CHARACTER was very popular in most western movies and novels: the Indian fighter. He had scars and stories to attest to his run-ins with Indians. Indian fighters knew everything about Indians, from "Indian law" to arrow design, and they were capable of engaging two to three Indians in hand-to-hand combat—all at one time—and emerge the victor. In the old West, technically speaking, anyone who fought against Indians, win or lose, was an Indian fighter. On the other hand, there were Indians who fought whites, but for whatever reason, the label white-man fighter never caught on in movies and novels.

Indian fighters, as it turned out, never really went away. They had simply lain low for several decades. They reemerged in the 1940s and 1950s. Instead of rifles, pistols, or sabers, their weapons were programs and policies aimed at solving the "Indian problem."

There were problems in Indian country: inadequate health care, loss of land, school dropouts, substandard housing, and racial discrimination, to list a few. Indians blamed the U.S. government and white society in general. The other side generally attributed the basis for the Indian problem to a lack of a work ethic, overlooking the fact that jobs were scarce on Indian reservations.

One of the frequent proposed solutions was to bring native people into the white mainstream, rationalizing that it was time for them to divest themselves of the federal dole and make it on their own—like everyone else. This would have to involve, of course, legislation that would terminate reservations. That would free up millions of acres of land, something that native tribes and nations did not want.

The attitude of termination would help form U.S. Indian policy for the decades of the fifties and sixties. A series of governmental resolutions would reach deep into the lives of native people. One of them was the Voluntary Relocation Program, known simply to the people it affected as "Relocation." It was implemented through the BIA.

Relocation did exactly that. It relocated native people from their reservations to large cities such as Minneapolis, Denver, Los Angeles, Cleveland, and Chicago. The objective was to put natives in an urban setting where jobs were plentiful, and native families would have the opportunity to fit into the "mainstream" of American life. Part of the consequence, however, was confusion and culture shock.

The Lakota had their share of families who were literally on the reservation one day and in a big city the next. Most were reluctant to leave home, and their uncertainty was exacerbated by false promises about the living conditions in their destination cities. Many families stayed in the new environment for only a few days before they headed home, although others tried to make the situation work. Proponents and administrators of the program, as well as the participants, did not take into consideration the adverse psychological impact of the radical change in environment. Lakota families were accustomed to rural settings or small towns, and they found it difficult to set up housekeeping in a tiny apartment in the middle of a crowded city. It was a faster-paced lifestyle they had never imagined. For many it was their first time away from home and their extended families, and most of the participants had never been near a city in their lives. So when they found themselves in poor, slumlike housing, or a job did not materialize, or their wages were low, or the work environment was unsupportive or even hostile, the only logical course was to go back home. Overall, Relocation did not work for everyone.

A common reaction from employers and BIA personnel was to blame the Indians. Relocated families wanted the opportunity to make a good living for their families. That was their main motivation for signing on for Relocation, because there simply were not enough jobs on the reservations.

Between one third and one half of all native families who tried Relocation, Lakota included, returned home. According to them, the best that could be said for Relocation is that it finally ended. In retrospect, it might have been a last-ditch attempt at assimilation, even though the idea of natives becoming "productive members" of mainstream America has not faded away completely.

Relocation, however, was not the U.S. government's only effort to solve the Indian problem in the 1950s, not for the Lakota, in any case. Public Law 280 would prove to be problematic in a different way.

Bypassing the consent of any tribes affected, P. L. 280 gave several states civil and criminal jurisdiction over Indian reservations. In the mid 1960s, the South Dakota reservations were not surprised when a referendum was held to decide the issue. Fortunately and wisely, the reservations banded together and organized a campaign. Assuming civil and criminal jurisdiction was not only a legal issue, the tribes contended. It would also be an economic issue because the federal government could not be counted on to pay for *state* jurisdiction. Consequently, the state's non-Indian citizens turned down civil and criminal jurisdiction over the reservations.

The tribal governments and Lakota, Dakota, and Nakota people in South Dakota could not predict the outcome of the referendum on jurisdiction. There was obviously immense relief when it was defeated. Civil and criminal jurisdiction would have adversely affected tribal sovereignty, and that would definitely have opened the door to other actions by the state and federal governments designed to weaken the tribes legally, and in every other way. The South Dakota tribes were aware of what had happened to the Menominee of Wisconsin just a few years before.

The U.S. Congress terminated the federal relationship with the Menominee and sixty other tribes. The affected tribes lost educational, health, and social services. But the loss of *trust* status of their lands made them subject to local property taxes. That is, the land was no longer legally federal land and they could be taxed. Many Menominee tribal members could not afford to pay the taxes, and they lost their lands. Although the Menominee had a lumber business because of the vast amounts of timber on their lands, it suffered setbacks and only added to their woes.

The federal action of termination was justified as an opportunity for the Menominee, and the other tribes affected, to release them from federal interference. But another motive came to light. Private interests desperately wanted the thousands of acres of timber on Menominee lands, and they leaned on Congress to push through the termination. Although significant lands had been lost, the Menominee, with nonnative support, requested restoration of trust status for their remaining lands to protect them. The request was not honored until 1974.

The tribes in South Dakota (and elsewhere) were painfully aware of the Menominee situation. They had not forgotten how the "peace talkers" of the United States had somehow forced an agreement to procure the gold rich Black Hills in 1875. During the 1940s, bills were regularly introduced in the U.S. Congress to terminate reservations. Fortunately, none were enacted until the Menominee timber became a prized commodity. Sixty other tribes were included to hide the underlying motive. But termination was the frequent cry through the halls of Congress, and no tribe was safe as long as they had land left within the exterior boundaries of their reservations.

Thus the new generation of Indian fighters emerged, dressed in pin-striped suits and carrying briefcases.

If it were not for land, timber, and mineral resources on reservations, natives would have been more of an invisible minority than we were from 1900 to the 1960s. The only other people having any consistent contact with Indians were whites on or near reservations. Beyond that, governmental entities with any awareness that Indians still existed were states with federal or state reservations inside their borders, and the federal government. At that level, the basic point of contact was the Department of the Interior, which contained the Bureau of Indian Affairs. In 1955, the Indian Health Service was established within the Department of Health, Education, and Welfare (now Health and Human Services). The U.S. Army Corps of Engineers had contact with tribes along the upper Missouri River when hydroelectric dams were planned and constructed. From the mid-1960s, the Department of Housing and Urban Development became very familiar with tribes because of various reservation housing projects. Of course, congressional representatives from those states with reservations were also familiar with native peoples.

The majority of the American mainstream, meanwhile, did not know much about them. Information was obtained mostly from history books and other scholarly works, novels, television, and movies. But most did not have a need or desire to know about native people and their culture and history. After World War II, Americans were aware that nearly thirty thousand Indians had served in all branches of the service. Some were draftees, but most were volunteers. Those who served alongside them knew that fact firsthand, and, of course, the stories of the Navajo code talkers in the Pacific theater of operations made the rounds. Not many Americans are aware, even today, that there were code talkers from other tribes, such as the Comanche and Lakota, who performed the same service in the European theater. But native people fighting and dying in the military service of the United States did little overall to change their social and economic status.

Most whites on or near reservations and civil service employees at the state or federal levels commonly regarded Indians as a subjugated or conquered people. All legal and social interaction was on that basis.

Lack of awareness about natives meant that the general public, the mainstream, did not know the social and economic conditions natives confronted day in and day out. If there was any sense about what was happening in "Indian country," it was that they were being "taken care of" by the federal government. But that was not the case. Poor housing, minimal health care, a high dropout rate for Indian students, and lack of employment was the reality. Ironically, those factors were used by the federal government as justification for assimilation and termination. Mainstreaming Indians, rather than dealing with the problems, seemed to be the preferred answer to the "Indian problem." The federal government would take a closer look at those problems, and awareness of those issues would be brought before the American public. But not until native peoples themselves took action.

After World War II, people from the various tribes began migrating to cities. Their reasons were much the same as every other American's in the postwar era. They were looking for opportunities for a better economic life, at the very least. Many hoped that the cities would be a better place to raise families as well. The Relocation program had lived up to its name and sent more, so by the 1960s most large cities had pockets of native communities. Unfortunately for many urban natives, the economic and social realities of cities forced them into the same kinds of hardships faced by their relatives on the reservations: inadequate or no health care, poor housing, and racism, among others.

While those natives who remained on reservations at least had some semblance of assistance from the BIA and the Indian Health Service, no such system was specifically available for those in the urban areas. They were lumped into the same lower economic and social categories as other minorities and poor whites. These circumstances and consequences were not what native families had had in mind when they'd uprooted themselves from their reservation roots.

The state of native communities, both on and off the reservation, was not good in the 1960s. An entire nation was facing several touchy issues in the early part of the decade, including civil rights and the Vietnam conflict. Civil rights had been an issue for native people long before it boiled over nationally for African Americans. A few elected native leaders on the reservations tried to address social and economic issues, but their complaints fell on deaf ears in a government that still chose to adopt a paternal stance where anything associated with native people was concerned. Urban natives were complaining as well, but out of their dissatisfaction grew what was regarded by many mainstream Americas as a new mind-set for natives: activism.

The new activism had a name: the American Indian Movement (AIM). AIM was founded in 1968 in Minneapolis, Minnesota. Its creation is directly attributed to police harassment of Indians in Minneapolis and St. Paul. Frequent complaints and appeals to civic leaders had brought no satisfactory solutions. Consequently, natives formed patrols to observe the police. From its inception, AIM knew about bad situations. The organization called attention to as many of them as it could that affected native people, whether in the city or on the reservation. But AIM gained its greatest notoriety from its clash with police in Custer, South Dakota, and the seventy-one-day siege at Wounded Knee in 1973.

Custer was a consequence of white authorities' opting not to prosecute the white killer of a young Lakota man, Wesley Bad Heart Bull. AIM protested and fought with local and state police. The incident overshadowed the reason it occurred, and in all likelihood firmly established AIM as proponents of violence in the minds of most Americans who had seen the television news reports. AIM's occupation of the village of Wounded Knee solidified that characterization.

As tensions escalated as a result of the murder of young Bad Heart Bull, the tribal administration at Pine Ridge banned AIM from the reservation. The tribal chairman had been unresponsive to concerns of traditional Lakota and was suspected of corruption. AIM stood firmly on the side of the traditional community. BIA officials, fearing more violence, requested that federal marshals be sent to the Pine Ridge Reservation.

AIM's reaction was to occupy the little town of Wounded Knee, the site of the massacre of 1890. The federal government's reaction was to send in its contingent of "Indian fighters," armed to the teeth.

Scores of U.S. marshals, complete with armored personnel carriers, were sent to Wounded Knee. By the time the siege was over, they had fired over half a million rounds at AIM's barricaded compound. Two occupants of Wounded Knee were killed, and several were wounded.

Sadly, Indian fighters turned up when least expected. James Abourezk and George McGovern were the senators from South Dakota. Abourezk worked tirelessly to bring both sides together to negotiate. Though involved in the process, McGovern did suggest that the issue be left up to the "good citizens" of South Dakota. That statement apparently did not include the occupiers of Wounded Knee within the characterization of "good citizens."

Many Lakota, Dakota, and Nakota people in South Dakota voted to elect McGovern to the Senate, and supported his bid for the presidency. Many of them were surprised, given McGovern's favorable stance on native issues, as well as his assuming the mantle of a "peace candidate," that he seemed more punitive than peaceful where Wounded Knee was concerned. He seemed to regard the takeover as an unlawful and defiant act, without truly considering the circumstances that had facilitated it. In any case, there was a feeling in the Indian community in South Dakota (and elsewhere) that his true feelings toward Indians had emerged. Many Lakota, Dakota, and Nakota people were deeply disappointed and, in some cases, heartbroken.

White ethnocentric attitudes of the nineteenth century had fueled the drive to take Lakota lands. One such attitude was the feeling that the Euro-American nation was entitled to the land because of its needs and superiority as a civilized society. In the twentieth century, paternalistic federal and state attitudes and policies were an extension of those first attitudes, which went on to become the foundation for the social and economic conditions for the native people on the northern plains, and elsewhere, in the 1960s. Activism, at the very least, was a necessary counterpoint to Indian fighters.

The activism that rose to the top in the 1960s was nothing new. Many Lakota were aware of their history. They were aware that white attitudes of the nineteenth century had continued into the twentieth. The attitudes, policies, and actions of the U.S. government in the latter half of the nineteenth century were motivation for men like Sitting Bull and Crazy Horse to take action against them. But as negative attitudes were passed from one generation to the next, so was resistance to them. Resistance in the twentieth century was labeled by the white establishment and many in the media as militancy, with the assumption that it happened because "militants" were against anything white. AIM's activism and "militancy" did not merely attempt to call attention to serious problems. Its actions were also a sincere effort to facilitate solutions. For example, when American colonists—dressed as natives, no less—dumped containers of tea in Boston Harbor in protest against high taxes imposed by their mother country, their action was characterized as heroic and patriotic and *necessary*.

They were calling attention to issues they believed were detrimental to their well-being. Lakota activism, and Indian activism in general, stood on the same principle. Whatever most Lakota and other native peoples thought of the violence AIM became involved in, deep in their hearts they agreed that bad situations existed for them and applauded the American Indian Movement for taking a stand.

Though its public profile is somewhat lower, AIM still exists. Over its thirty-seven year history it has been involved in establishing many programs dear to the hearts of Indians everywhere, such as the Legal Rights Center for Indians, the International Indian Treaty Council, and Women of All Red Nations (WARN). If its destiny was to focus public attention on issues of deep concern to native people all over the country, AIM has certainly fulfilled it. That it was unable to facilitate meaningful resolutions to the issues raised in 1968 by leading consistent and meaningful dialogue may have been due to its early penchant for violent confrontation as much as the other side's unwillingness to listen. Nevertheless, while AIM may be regarded by some as a failed experiment in activism, its legacy is a statement that activism was, and still is, necessary.

Especially as long as Indian fighters are still around.

NINETEEN

The Twenty-first Century

*Like the Miners' Canary, the Indian marks the shift from
fresh air to poison gas in our political atmosphere.*

—Felix Cohen

IN THE PAST, the Lakota told their age by citing the number of
winters they had lived: *"Waniyetu wikcemna sakowin wanni,"* or
"I have lived seventy winters," for example. Winter was, and is,
the toughest season of the year on the northern plains. It is still
common for Lakota speakers to tell their age in this way.

The turn of a new century is a critically significant milestone.
In a real sense, it means that the Lakota have made it through another winter, one over a hundred years long and fraught with
challenges. And as the first few years of the twenty-first century
slide by, many Lakota face it with a determination not to forget
what they have experienced and endured to have arrived at this
point in time. It is a determination born of the hard-won sense of
identity that has survived that long winter of challenge after challenge. They have not forgotten who they are, and that is ar-
guably the most important individual and societal strength with
which to face challenges.

Facing the world, and life itself, from the perspective of who and what we are can be the greatest strength, because we are most comfortable in our own skin. Perhaps that is what men like Spotted Tail and Red Cloud were hoping and praying for when they advised the people to learn to live *like* the whites. Their message was misunderstood by some, but they were trying to say that living like white people did not necessarily mean *becoming* white. And in not becoming white it would be possible to remain Lakota as much as possible.

On the other hand, Sitting Bull and Crazy Horse fought hard to keep the Lakota nation free and intact. But in the end, they wanted what Spotted Tail and Red Cloud wanted: for the Lakota nation to endure, somehow.

The Lakota have endured, but not without some losses. The Lakota language is still spoken by about 30 percent of their population, a factor which less than 10 of the 480 or so ethnically identifiable native tribes in the United States can attest to. And much of their traditions, customs, beliefs, and values still remain.

Lakota lifestyle has changed, though, because the buffalo are gone. The hunter/warrior society is gone. There are no more communal buffalo chases, and it has been necessary to find other ways to survive. Casinos seem to be a way for Lakota tribes to cash in, but unfortunately the degree of largesse is dependent on the number of people who walk through the doors of a casino to gamble. Tribes in sparsely populated rural areas have a thin profit margin, if any at all. Furthermore, if the states and the federal government have their way, casinos will be regulated, taxed, and surcharged out of existence in a scenario not unlike white hide hunters decimating the buffalo herds.

But like other native tribes, the Lakota are survivors. And they have the ability to adapt without changing the core essence

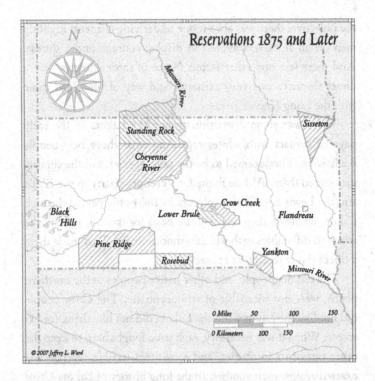

Reservations 1875 and Later

N

Missouri River

Standing Rock

Sisseton

Cheyenne
River

Black
Hills

Crow Creek

Lower Brule

Flandreau

Pine Ridge

Yankton

Rosebud

Missouri River

0 Miles 50 100 150
0 Kilometers 100 150

© 2007 Jeffrey L. Ward

of who and what they are. If that ability is taught to each succeeding generation, there will always be Lakota people in the world. But it will be necessary to adapt to different kinds of enemies.

There was a time when the Crow, occasionally the Blackfeet, Shoshoni, Arikara, and the Pawnee were Lakota enemies. The Lakota met them on the field of battle, and the rules of engagement were simple: Whoever fought the hardest and with the most skill was the victor. Success or victory did not always depend on body count, however. More often it was the recovery of horses or captives, or the satisfaction of revenge. But whatever the objective, there was always one underlying element: Fighting men on all sides endeavored to display courage under duress. And there was one other factor: None of those enemies were a direct threat to our very existence and way of life. That came with the Long Knives.

There was some discussion among the Lakota in the early days of contact with whites regarding what those new people really were. They seemed to be the same species, but the similarities ended there. Although the La Vérendrye party in the 1720s and the Lewis and Clark explorers in 1804 only passed through Lakota territory, they revealed the basis for most, if not all, the eventual difficulties with whites: ethnocentrism. That made them a direct threat to Lakota existence.

The Lakota people, and other native peoples in the northern plains, were not incapable of ethnocentrism. The Crow people did not like the Lakota, and the Lakota did not like them, for example. When it was necessary, each tribe fought hard to keep the other out of its territories, and sometimes terrible revenge was exacted against each another. In the long history of Lakota-Crow conflict, neither side was always victorious against the other. But each, to the other, was like the whetstone that sharpens the blade; each side had to remain strong in order to contend with the other, and consequently, there was mutual respect between enemies.

Enemies, such as the Crow and the Shoshoni, were considered worthy adversaries, and sometimes they were characterized as tricky or sneaky. But rarely were they characterized as having no honor.

On the other hand, it was difficult to categorize the white man, because he was in so many ways outside the context of how the

Lakota defined their existence and their world. Therefore, there was no small debate over whether or not the white man was an enemy in the same class as the Crow, Shoshoni, Omaha, Blackfeet, Arikara, and others. But as time went on and the Lakota realized the extreme threat posed by the white man, he was regarded as an enemy unlike any ever encountered. To some, the white man was more like a scourge than an enemy.

Nearly 280 years after La Vérendrye and 200 hundred years after Lewis and Clark, their kind of ethnocentrism remains, confirming that assessment. Indeed, many things have changed, but many are the same. For example:

- In the decades of the 1940s, 1950s, and 1960s, Lakota high school students on the verge of graduating were encouraged to attend trade school instead of college. Many followed this advice and found ways to make a living as carpenters, heavy-equipment operators, cooks, electricians, and automobile mechanics. However, the basic rationale used by white teachers and counselors at public, government, and parochial schools for dispensing this type of career guidance was that Indians were *good with their hands*. The implication, of course, was that Lakota students were not good with their minds.

- Although the Lakota population in the state of South Dakota is a fraction less than 10 per cent of the total, there are just over nine hundred Lakota inmates in the state penitentiary, out of a total population of thirty-five hundred, or about 26 percent (as of early 2006).

- Throughout the state, Lakota citizens expect extra scrutiny from law enforcement officers, as well as less-than-courteous professional treatment. A few years ago, the commissioner of Indian affairs for the state of South Dakota, a Lakota appointed by the governor, was stopped and questioned by officers as he jogged in a public city park.

• In the early 1980s, the city fathers of Aberdeen South Dakota, revealed their attitudes about Indian money. The Bureau of Indian Affairs (in the Department of the Interior) and the Indian Health Service (in the Department of Health and Human Services) have had their regional offices in Aberdeen for decades. Regional offices (formerly area offices) are the administrative and technical assistance programs between the agency or reservation level and the national headquarters in Washington, D.C. Each employs hundreds of people, which means a payroll in the millions of dollars annually spent in the city and immediate area, not to mention the ancillary services that both the BIA and IHS buy and pay for. In the early 1980s, the Indian Health Service wanted to move its offices and its annual budget to Rapid City, but there was opposition to the move, and not from the tribes in the three-state area. Political leaders and concerned citizens gathered all the support they could find to keep the Indian Health Service in Aberdeen. The state's congressional representatives helped champion Aberdeen's cause, and the IHS officials eventually succumbed to the pressure. Overlooked or ignored was the Indian Health Service plan to refurbish facilities it already owned in Rapid City. In the long term, the relocation would have saved millions of taxpayer dollars, because the IHS would not have had to pay to lease its own buildings. It is understandable that no one would want to lose millions of dollars from the local economy. But the dark side to the episode—rarely mentioned—was that the area director of the Indian Health Service, and her family, were subjected to threats and attacks on their property because she was doing her job as the point person in discussing and planning the move.

Similar attitudes exist in communities in and around reservations. The Bureau of Indian Affairs functions at the reservation level, maintaining administrative as well as operational personnel. Annual budgets range from a few million and higher. The Indian Health Service also maintains clinics and hospitals on the reservations. Their budgets are similar.

The greater percentage of the disposable income of those civil service employees is spent in the area, so businesses on or near reservations benefit, especially those that provide essential products and services, such as automobile dealerships, food markets, gasoline stations, propane and heating-oil and utility companies.

Tribal governments also provide programs and services to their tribal members and have dozens and sometimes hundreds of employees. Furthermore, tribes, the Indian Health Service, and the Bureau of Indian Affairs at the reservation level buy products and services from local vendors as well. In short, funding by tribal members pours millions of dollars into businesses on or near reservations. But most of those businesses are owned by people who are not native.

The Lakota can only try to endure the circumstances that caused the incidents described. Change can come only if the individuals or groups that perpetrate such behavior stop themselves and if the society they are part of no longer condones such actions and attitudes.

However the Lakota perceive themselves, and however the rest of America perceives them, we are all here together in the twenty-first century. The Lakota today are known more commonly as the Pine Ridge Sioux, Rosebud Sioux, Cheyenne River Sioux, Standing Rock Sioux, and Lower Brule Sioux. Those labels, if nothing else, hint at the road they have traveled thus far—a road strewn with broken treaties, gold rushes, redefined boundaries, a shrinking land base, boarding schools, misguided legislation, racism, paternalism, misperception, and sometimes plain bad luck. But as one old Lakota man suggested in the early 1960s, "We probably brought it on ourselves when we showed up for the 1851 Fort Laramie Treaty Council." In his opinion, the Lakota empowered the whites when that happened, and that power was solidified when the first Lakota headman scratched an X on the paper beside his name. The old man felt that no one should have shown up at Fort Laramie. Since the whites already had designs on Lakota lands, the Lakota should not have given the process any credibility. In his estimation, his Lakota ancestors were too polite.

The overwhelming majority of Lakota today either have a non-Lakota surname, or family names are spoken and written in English. While it is laudable that at least 30 percent speak Lakota, the other part of that reality is that about 70 percent do not. And although the legislative bodies for tribal governments are called councils, there ends the similarity to what councils were in prereservation days. As a matter of fact, since 1934 and the Indian Reorganization Act, tribal councils have been conducting business under the authority of the U.S. government, and not because they are empowered as a function of Lakota society. As a Lakota attorney has said: "Self-government by permission is not self-government at all. . . ."

All in all, this is part of the way things are for the Lakota today, and they accept it. Winter has a way of culling. The road they have traveled for nearly three hundred years has exacted some losses. But they have survived to this point. They remember who their ancestors were, and to a great extent they still know who they are. They will pass on the culture to the next generation, even though it will happen mostly in English. There are, however, efforts underway to revive the Lakota language and increase the percentage of native speakers.

The Lakota accept the way things are not because they like the way things are, but because they have the ability to strengthen themselves. It is entirely possible that Lakota tribal councils will again be the repositories of wisdom rather than hotbeds of factional politics. It is entirely possible that in a few generations, 70 percent of the Lakota population will be speaking Lakota.

As a people and as a nation, the Lakota have survived many winters, and they will survive many more. And they will pause frequently to remember the lessons learned in that process of survival. There is one lesson, perhaps no more or no less important than any other, but it is one they will endeavor to keep uppermost in their minds and firmly in their hearts. It is a lesson for all people, all societies, and all nations: When an enemy throws the worst it can at us, we must meet it with the best we have.

EPILOGUE

The Victors' Road

THE BATTLE OF THE LITTLE BIGHORN has long been regarded as a pivotal event, often *the* pivotal event, in the history of the Lakota, Dakota, and Nakota people, not to mention the Northern Cheyenne and Northern Arapaho. But to regard it as the primary cause for the consequences suffered by its victors at the hands of the U.S. government is wrong.

According to the ultimatum issued by the United States, all Lakota and Northern Cheyenne people were to report to reservations by January 31, 1876. President Ulysess Grant and his advisers, primarily generals Sherman and Sheridan, knew full well that the order would be ignored. That did not matter to them. What did matter was that the ultimatum gave them the legal authority to launch a "pacification campaign."

The ultimatum was ignored, although not because the Lakota were defying the authority of the United States. Most of the Lakota people were not aware of it, and although leaders such as Sitting Bull and Crazy Horse eventually got the drift of it primarily through the rumors passed on by Lakota already on reservations, it meant nothing to them. In their reality, the Long Knives had no authority over them that needed to be defied. However, we now see the state of their situation at that moment: Sitting Bull and Crazy Horse and their followers regarded themselves as free people with the right to live as they chose.

If the Battle of the Little Bighorn had been a victory for the U.S. Seventh Cavalry, it would have been an expected part of the pacification campaign. And if Custer had split his forces in that scenario and won, he probably would have been called a genius. But in real life he split his command and lost. Consequently, he is vilified for not following orders because he did not wait for General Terry, for attacking prematurely, and for further tempting fate by splitting his forces. Custer's defeat and death became an opportunity to win public support. Now the government *had* to subjugate the Lakota for what happened at the Little Bighorn. That was the rallying point. The "Indian wars" became something of a holy war because American blood had been spilled in the cause of Manifest Destiny. Uncivilized minions had blasphemed civilization. There was nothing to be done but punish in the name of righteousness.

It is entirely possible, of course, that President Grant and General Sherman and General Sheridan sent Custer back to his unit to be part of Terry's command, knowing that he was capable of some type of sensational act, either a sensational victory or a sensational disaster. Either way, he would serve a purpose.

The shocking defeat of an "elite" unit at the hands of "savages" barely out of the Stone Age creates a glare that obscures the reality of the big picture. The United States was out to gather up the last free-roaming bands of Lakota and Northern Cheyenne, no matter what.

The Lakota world did end at the Little Bighorn because of the government's intent to end it, not because we won a great victory. But that day was the culmination of any number of days that might have been the beginning of the end over the course of several generations. It might have been the day the French explorers led by the sieur de la Vérendrye first laid coveting eyes on the northern plains, or the day someone took to heart Captain William Clark's angry suggestion to force the Lakota into a dependence on the government's will. Or perhaps it was the day a white man discovered gold in the Black Hills. Or any of the days a peace talker drafted a treaty that was more favorable to his side. Or the day ethnocentric arrogance declared the West to have land free for the taking.

But we must ask ourselves, as Lakota people looking back on our history, what did come to an end at the Little Bighorn? The answer to that question would likely vary, depending on who addresses it. Crazy Horse and Sitting Bull wanted to maintain the hunting lifestyle, but in all likelihood, they realized that some influence from white culture was unavoidable.

Crazy Horse was promised his own agency in what is now north central Wyoming, in the Powder River region he loved so much. On that agency he probably fully expected to be able to live in much the same way he always had, knowing there would be boundaries he would have to acknowledge. But as long as lodges could be pitched and he could ride off into the hills, he would have accepted those boundaries. The reality of agency life was a shock to him and his people once they arrived at Fort Robinson, Nebraska—especially when Crazy Horse and some of his young men were forced to wait for permission from the U.S. government to go on a buffalo hunt. That permission was never given.

Crazy Horse probably would have adapted to agency life if for no other reason than that he was well aware his example was the road for others to follow. Sitting Bull did adapt to reservation life after he came back from Canada. After that, curiosity prompted him to join the Buffalo Bill Wild West Show. After he returned, he disdained going to the agency headquarters at Fort Yates, North Dakota, demonstrating enough passive-aggressive behavior to irk the Indian agent James McLaughlin. He simply wanted McLaughlin to know that he was no "loafer" agency Indian willing to stand in the issue line for a paltry ration of beans and rice. He was willing to acquiesce to reservation life, but as much on his own terms as possible.

Both Sitting Bull and Crazy Horse knew full well that the old buffalo-hunting days were over. The lifestyle that had defined who and what they were was gone. The world they loved, the world they preferred, had come to an end, and it was very difficult to bear. But they were also wise enough to realize that they had to try in every way possible to adapt and survive. Sadly, as we are fully aware, circumstances did not allow either of them to do that.

Since we Lakota are able to look back from the perspective of the twenty-first century, we are obviously not extinct as a people. We modern Lakota have not lived the buffalo-hunting lifestyle. As much as some, or perhaps many of us, know of it, we have not been there. We only know intellectually what was lost. We only know intellectually what our ancestors had to endure in order to adapt to a new lifestyle. But we should be fully aware that we are the manifestation of that change. We are here because our grand-parents, great-grandparents, and great-great-grandparents faced and endured forced change with their strength: the virtues and beliefs that had sustained them as Lakota people. They endured the end of their world to ensure that there would be a Lakota na-tion to emerge from that trauma.

The Battle of the Little Bighorn was not the reason our

world came to an end. But it did reaffirm for us that we were a strong nation quite capable of defending ourselves. We, and our Northern Cheyenne friends, were the victors at Little Bighorn. Non-Indian historians will admit that, but in the same breath remind us that we did lose the war. Among us there is a notion that the "war" is not over. Someday, perhaps, we will celebrate another victory, but not a victory won by fighting men with rifles and bows and arrows. Someday we will celebrate a victory of the spirit because the forces that sent armies to herd our ancestors onto reservations could not destroy the essence of our culture.

A celebration has been observed for 130 years and counting, although those who dance in celebration today may not know the exact reason it started. When word of the victory at the Little Bighorn reached the Red Cloud and Spotted Tail agencies, there was a mixture of dread and rejoicing. Many people were afraid that retribution would fall first and most heavily on the Lakota living on the agencies. Yet there was also a sense of pride.

The Sicangu Lakota organized a small victory celebration later in the autumn, away from the prying eyes of Indian police and soldiers. However, the following year, after they had relocated to the north in their ancestral homeland west of the Missouri River, they decided to celebrate again. So they danced to honor their warriors who had been in the battle. Someone produced a tattered flag, probably a cavalry guidon captured at the battle. It was a symbol of that victory, so a warrior was selected to carry it as he led the dance.

That celebration still occurs, but it is now known as the Rosebud Sioux Tribal Fair and Powwow. Many of the Sicangu Lakota (Rosebud Sioux), as well as other native peoples and non-Indians who attend the fair regularly, probably do not know that they are part of the longest, continuous commemoration of a single event.

At the Rosebud Fair, as well as at many other Lakota celebrations and powwows, there is a recurring ceremony. Lakota military veterans lead the grand entrance at the opening of each day or evening's dancing. They carry the American flag and tribal flags into the dance arena. Many native veterans from various tribes are proud of their service in the military branches of our country. That is one reason they carry the American flag, but there is another reason.

A flag was captured at the Battle of the Little Bighorn, in fact, several flags. Among them are company guidons and the 1876 version of the American flag. At a victory dance after the battle, those captured flags were carried by warriors who had fought and defeated the soldiers. Sometime later, at celebrations across Lakota country, American flags were carried and displayed—but not as symbols of pride for the nation they represented. They were displayed as trophies of war, a reminder of victory. Most important, they were displayed to honor the men who had fought, and died, in that victory.

It would be somewhat anticlimactic for Little Bighorn to be nothing more than a place or a battle. Nothing happens without purpose, whether it is obvious or we apply a purpose and meaning. Little Bighorn was a turning point for us historically and culturally. Life not only changed, it also got tougher. Black Elk, a friend and contemporary of Crazy Horse's, summed it up this way:

> The Washichus have put us in these square boxes, our power is gone and we are dying, for the power is not in us anymore. You can look at our boys and see how it is with us. When we were living by the power of the circle in the way

we should, boys were men at twelve or thirteen. But now it takes them very much longer to mature. Well, it is as it is. We are prisoners of war while we are waiting here. But there is another world.

Black Elk spoke of the harsh reality of life on the reservation and its effects. But he also saw that the circumstances the Lakota were in, no matter how difficult—and because they were difficult—would help them find or make something better.

We should always remember Little Bighorn as a significant part of our history, and we should always celebrate the victory our ancestors achieved there. Their victory was a source of strength and inspiration as the victors found themselves in the turmoil of change. They remembered they could be strong and taught their sons and daughters that strength could be manifested in many different ways. Strength flowed, therefore, from one generation to the next, and survival became victory. But each generation has to honor the one before.

After the turn of the twentieth century, canvas tipis pitched next to log houses were common sights on Lakota reservations. They represented a tug-of-war that was becoming more and more of an issue. One old Lakota man explained his unwillingness to give up the round tipi. In that dwelling, he asserted, the white man's devil could not catch him in a corner.

By 1890, the log house was not new to the Lakota. Log and sod houses dotted the prairies. Frame houses were the usual domicile in towns and settlements. Square houses and buildings were as blatantly foreign to the Lakota as the people who built them, used them, and lived in them. The old Lakota man's remark may have been made in jest, but he did voice a very real fear. It was not the white man's devil he was afraid of, however; he was afraid of the white man himself.

Strangely enough, even under the most trying or awkward of circumstances, people from different backgrounds somehow find ways to connect. Friendships developed between white and Lakota individuals and families, frequently lasting a lifetime. In one small town in the northern part of the Rosebud Reservation, a white man took the trouble to learn Lakota. Consequently, he was quite popular because he could converse to some extent, and he had many friends in the Lakota community. If nothing else, he became a symbol, a hope, that not all white people were alike. He was not the only one, by any means, but people like him were few and far between.

But at the collective level, the white man's devil did come into play. Hanging over interpersonal relationships between Lakota and whites—like a hammer ready to strike—was the fact that whites were in control. Control wielded by the state and federal governments was the handle of the hammer. It fostered a sense of white racial superiority as well as an attitude of impunity. After all, the white people had "won" the so-called Indian wars, proving—at least to themselves—they were superior. And that superiority was manifested in every aspect of reservation life. White people were employed by the BIA, and white churches operated parochial boarding schools. The administrators who ran government boarding schools were white people, and so were the teachers and the people who ran the dormitories. White physicians treated Lakota illnesses and often ridiculed Lakota healers and healing practices. White Christian clergy loudly and steadfastly railed against the "pagan" and "heathen" Lakota spiritual beliefs and religious practices. And the stores and trading posts were owned and operated by white people.

The sense of impunity was the head of the hammer. White people could say and do just about anything to a Lakota, or about Lakota people, knowing that the system was on their side—right or wrong.

Therefore, while that old Lakota man likely had no real fear of white people as individuals, and may even have had a white friend or two, he was well aware of what white people had done as a group, and what they were still capable of doing as a group.

It was the stated duty of the BIA and its missionary partners to transform the Lakota into something better than they were. One can only wonder if the efforts would have stopped if every Lakota had denounced his culture, spoken English, and gone to church every Sunday. Perhaps not.

There were those among the Lakota who embraced the new order to the point of giving up their culture. This was not a new phenomenon. It first occurred in the 1850s, when individuals and sometimes entire family groups pitched their lodges within the shadows of white forts and settlements. One phrase that described them was *wasicu ob tipi,* or "those who live with the whites." Such phrases evolved into "loaf-about-the-forts," or simply "loafers" in English. Loafers were at first interested in the *things* white people had to offer, but eventually they saw no harm in adopting the ways of the whites. When this occurred in the early days of the reservations, therefore, it was not a total surprise.

Many Lakota men hired on as police, but most of them did so to support their families and to find a new sense of purpose. Hundreds enlisted in the army, and some were assigned to duty stations on reservations; others saw duty far away from home, such as during the Spanish-American War. Most of these men were not "loafers." Though their military service took them to places they never knew existed, most of them did not forsake their cultural identities for the sake of employment or adventure. In fact, to most Lakota, living like whites did not mean having to forsake their culture. Living like white people was necessary to survive and make a living within the reality of how things were. Inside of them still beat a Lakota heart.

But the forces of assimilation still worked hard, exhorting each and every Lakota to "better" himself or herself. In the 1940s and 1950s, boarding schools were still conscripting students. Every autumn, buses prowled the communities, and children—willing or not—were loaded on and hauled to school. There they were taught to "better" themselves. How, many Lakota wondered, can we be better than we are?

Indeed, the mantra spawned by the policy of administration, and which motivated the effort of many a government official, missionary, and teacher, was not often defined in so many words. Even into the 1960s, Lakota students were told that finishing high school was a way to "better" themselves. It was one of the, if not *the*, most insidiously racist statements made to native students anywhere.

Anyone who told any native to "better yourself" was not talking about native people pulling themselves up by the bootstraps from poverty to riches. They were talking about crossing over from native to white. They were saying that to leave behind—to put aside, to deny, or otherwise cast off—the burden of being Lakota, or any other native tribe, would be an upgrade in status as a human being.

The mantra was the anthem of every well-meaning or

mean-spirited social reformer who actually believed that native people would be better off as part of the mainstream society. And the effort put forth as a consequence of that firm belief did, unfortunately, cause confusion and heartache. Children were the easiest targets. Year after year in the boarding schools, from nearly every adult there, they heard continuous denigration of who and what they and their families were. It was only a matter of time before their loyalties collapsed. Any Lakota child that did not outright give in to the constant pressure entered a state of confusion that often lasted a lifetime. Many Lakota adults who attended boarding schools now have to fight the demons that nearly destroyed their sense of identity—demons that were, and are, a common vestige of the boarding school experience.

Lydia Whirlwind Soldier, a Lakota writer, poet, and educator, tells one of the most poignant and heartbreaking stories of the boarding school experience: her own. In *Shaping Survival: Essays by Four American Indian Tribal Women*, she writes:

> I have wrestled with telling my story because of the repercussions I expect from the Catholic community here on the Rosebud Reservation, but I have resolved not to spare the worst because I am writing my story for the children who suffered in the boarding schools. I speak for those children whose stories will never be told, for those of us who still suffer from post-traumatic stress, for the lost generations who stand on the street corners and dig in trash cans for aluminum cans to sell, for those who deaden their pain with alcohol and drugs, and for their families who have suffered from generational grief

and invisible scars. Finally, I speak for those who have lost their culture and heritage and have not seen it as a loss.

In the summer when Lydia was four years old, a man in a dusty car came to her family's house in the Bad Nation community. Lydia, her six-year-old brother, and five-year-old cousin were hauled off to boarding school. Lydia spoke no English. At the school, after an introduction to a stern woman in a dormitory, she began her formal education.

This was only the beginning. In the next few years, until I learned to speak English correctly, I would be treated as if I were retarded or hard of hearing. The people who ran the school thought that the louder they spoke, the better I would understand, so at times all communication was conducted in shouting voices.

In the third grade, Lydia met a teacher who was determined to do anything to teach her to speak English correctly. Her favorite method was a red switch—a whip. And if that did not work, a closet became the next motivator.

My spirit was beaten and tattered in the third grade. The first time she used the switch on me it caught me on an angle across my forehead and my eyelid. The swelling nearly closed my eye. I fought against being put in the closet, crying silent tears as I was overpowered and locked in. I struggled to breathe in the inky darkness; it was difficult because of the dusty chalk smell. I sank to the floor, and lay there trying to breathe. I put my nose next to the crack at the bottom of the door and drew in shallow breaths trying not to draw the chalk dust into my lungs as I went to sleep. I knew that even if I prayed there was no one there to save me: my captors were the representatives of God.

Lydia Whirlwind Soldier's story is not an isolated case. As she so succinctly states, she speaks for those children whose stories will never be told. It is no wonder, then, that for as long as possible after Wounded Knee, tipis stood next to small square houses on all the Lakota reservations. Our Lakota ancestors were loath to relinquish the past. That the past was as difficult as it was glorious was not the issue. The past was where they were still, in every possible way, Lakota.

Many of those tipis stood season after season, patched and repatched until the canvas was too tattered and the poles too old to stay straight. Once the tipi was gone, the memory of it became and remained as real as the physicality of it. If our Lakota ancestors were loath to let go of the tipi, the heartbreak of their children and grandchildren hauled away to boarding schools was an indescribable pain.

Formal education, fortunately, has taken on a different and more positive meaning for the Lakota. It is a change that was spearheaded by the Lakota, Dakota, and Nakota. Beginning in the early 1970s, native colleges have been established on several of the reservations, and Lakota, Dakota, and Nakota communities have taken control over schools that formerly were operated by the BIA or by churches.

The first two Lakota colleges in South Dakota were on the

Rosebud and Pine Ridge reservations in the early 1970s: Sinte
Gleska College (named in honor of Spotted Tail) at Rosebud and
Oglala Lakota College on the Pine Ridge. Sisseton-Wahpeton
Community College on the Sisseton reservation, Sitting Bull Col-
lege on the Standing Rock, Si Tanka College (named in honor of
Big Foot) on the Cheyenne River Reservation, and Ihanktunwan
Community College on the Yankton reservation. All of these in-
stitutions were established for two primary reasons: to preserve
language and culture and to provide post-secondary education on
the reservations.

The passage of Public Law 93-638, the Indian Self-
determination and Education Assistance Act of 1975, has provided Lakota, Dakota, and Nakota communities and parents
more of a voice in the education of their children by giving them
control over some categories of federal funds for public schools,
and by enabling them to take operational and administrative
control over schools operated by the BIA. As a result, the cur-
riculum in those schools now includes courses in native history,
language, and culture.

Education was once the primary weapon of assimilation wielded
in the intensive and extensive effort to take away Lakota, Dakota,
and Nakota culture. Now it is the primary tool in the effort to
maintain it.

If formal education did not come gently to the reservations,
neither did Christianity. It came with a heavy hand and a hard
heart. Perhaps some of the missionary zeal has tempered over the
years. And perhaps some among the people who spread their
gospel now think that "renouncing the devil and all his works"
still means killing the Indian to save the man. But that intent and

all its consequent efforts did not succeed before, and it will not succeed in the future. There are many Lydia Whirlwind Soldiers who will tell their stories, and those stories will transcend the cruel and barbaric treatment Lakota students suffered in the name of assimilation. Those stories will be the strength of the Lakota people, because they will remind us that stinging switches and darkened closets could not extinguish the Lakota soul.

Many Lakota people have embraced Christianity, but not because its message is new. Many of the core values and philosophies it espouses—respect for parents, compassion, love of family, devotion to prayer, generosity, and fortitude—have been the basis of Lakota spiritual beliefs for countless generations. And in embracing Christianity, the Lakota people have demonstrated the one virtue that is often difficult for many people: forgiveness.

There are still those in the Christian community plagued by evangelical zeal who proclaim that natives should or must forsake their ethnicity to attain a higher station. Yet Lakota people who are Christians bring a deep faith to their commitment. That faith is, and was, part of their cultural heritage because their faith is in—God—*Wakantanka* and not in the often convoluted man-made doctrine associated with organized religion. Those people have not forsaken their ethnicity or cultural heritage. They are adding it to the mix, enriching the experience for everyone involved.

Be that as it may, some questions need to be asked. Have the policies and efforts of assimilation made the Lakota a better people? Have we forsaken our culture to climb to a higher place to be a "better" form of human being? Has the emotional and physical abuse heaped on Lakota children for several generations purged some part of us that does not measure up to the rest of the human species? The answer is a resounding *no*!

But there are at least two of many consequences that we must not forget. One, in spite of the fact that our sense of identity—language, customs, traditions, and values—was denounced, ridiculed, and attacked, we are still here as a viable culture. Second, assimilation did not teach us to *be* strong, it has taught us that we *are* strong. If either of these were not the case, there would be nothing left but unrecognizable versions of us in books written by nonnative scholars.

Yet there is another question that must also be asked. Are we the same?

The answer to that is also *no!*

We did not come through several generations of assimilation unscathed. While some of us still speak our language, most of us do not. Not all of us who are biologically Lakota are culturally Lakota. Not all of us know who we are, or know who we want to be.

But we should also be aware that much of the essence of the Lakota culture did survive, and we are passing it down in order to ensure that we still have a living language, traditional values, and a distinct identity. Enough has survived to enable us to guide others back to who and what they are.

So the image of the tipi next to a log cabin is one that should be taken quite seriously by those who were, and are, the targets of assimilation. It should also be taken seriously by those who were, and are, the instruments and enforcers of assimilation. It is not an ambiguous picture. A small part of it may represent acquiescence to change, but the larger part is resistance to it.

Change happens, even within a positive context. But when change is anticipated to be unwanted and painful, resistance to it rises in proportion. That is precisely the reason a stinging whip and a dark closet could not beat or frighten the essence of being Lakota out of a four-year-old Lakota girl. Most of the children in the government and parochial boarding schools who were horribly abused and punished for speaking Lakota followed the rules and refrained from speaking it on school grounds. Understandably, some of them were too deeply wounded to speak the language ever again. But most of them went back to speaking it for two reasons: One, it was an act of defiance, and two, while tragically the man or person can be killed, the essence of being Lakota cannot. In other words, no matter how determined assimilation was to kill the Indian to save the man, it did not happen. We are still here. And some of us still pitch tipis now and then.

We Lakota today are the descendants of the people encamped at the Little Bighorn in that summer of 1876. Some of us can trace our ancestry back to some who were there or who fought in the battle. But not all of us are fully aware of the meaning and significance of that time in our history. The Little Bighorn as a time and a place and an event is part of who and what we are. We owe it to our ancestors to know what happened there and in the years and generations that followed. We owe it to them because they were fighting and surviving for *us* just as much as they were for themselves.

We should celebrate their victory at the Little Bighorn, but we should also celebrate the strength of character each generation displayed thereafter. Without that strength, we Lakota would not be here today as a viable culture.

Without a doubt, the best way for us to celebrate our ancestors is never to forget who we are, and where we are from.

Mitukuyepi, nahanhci unlakotapelo. He kiksuyapo!

A Story: Remember

IN THE EARLY 1950s, a Lakota boy grew up with his grandparents and soon reached the age when his friends and relatives
were being sent off to school. Yet his grandparents kept the boy
home. Not until he was nearly nine did they allow him to go to
school.

From time to time, the boy wondered why his grandparents
had been reluctant for him to go to school. After he graduated
from high school, he finally asked his grandfather. The old man
did not answer specifically. He simply told a story.

*A certain man, a widower, and his only son lived alone along a river
on the land the father owned. The boy had a wonderful childhood
playing along the river and on the prairies all around. He attended a
one-room school a few miles away, and eventually went to a high
school in the nearest town. After high school, the boy wanted to go to
the university.*

*So his father sold most of the land he owned in order to pay for his
son's education, and he sent him off to a university a few hundred miles
away. During his first year, the boy wrote home every week, describing
to his father what the university was like. In the second year, the letters*

did not come as often, but he did write regularly. Since it was a journey of several hundred miles, the father knew he would have to wait a few more years to see his son. So he lived for his son's letters.

In the third year the letters came once or twice a month, and they were not as long as before. Many of them seemed to be dashed off in a hurry because the handwriting was difficult to read.

In the fourth year no letters came, and the father was distraught. He was afraid something might have happened to his son. Perhaps he is seriously ill, he imagined. Finally, when months passed without a single letter, the father—now getting older—could stand the loneliness no longer. He hitched up his team of horses to the buggy—his only means of transportation—and started the long journey to the university.

After many days of travel, he arrived at the university town. He walked among the buildings on the campus asking after his son. Days passed, but he could not find his son or anyone who knew him. The old man was a strange sight indeed, driving his horse-drawn buggy along streets filled with automobiles. After many days of fruitless searching, he finally decided to return home.

As he was leaving the campus, he drove by a large brick building. On its front steps was a tall and fine-looking young man dressed in a suit. He was speaking to a large crowd that was listening to every word. The old man immediately realized that the young man was his son!

Overjoyed and unable to contain himself, the old man leaped from his buggy and shoved his way through the crowd. He climbed the steps and embraced his son.

The young man pried himself from the old man's embrace. Looking down at the man dressed in old and tattered clothes, he stepped back. "Old man," he asked, "who are you? I do not know you."

The boy was shocked at his grandfather's story. "That's very sad," he observed.

"True," the grandfather replied, "but like all stories, it has a lesson. You can be like the young man in my story who forgot where he came from. Or you can choose never to forget who you are, and where you are from."

Resources

AS ALWAYS, much of the material regarding the Lakota perspective is from oral stories and information from Lakota people, not only about events such as the Battle of the Little Bighorn and the Wounded Knee Massacre, but also of their interesting, compelling, and often painful experiences in that often ignored period from 1890 to 1960. Many of those people were the first generation to be born on the reservations, and they willingly, but often reluctantly, shared their stories of what that period of transition was like for them. Most of those people have finished their earthly journey. I shall always be indebted to them.

Mitakuyepi, wopilia heca.

I am indebted for the use of excerpts from the essay written by Lydia Whirlwind Soldier, a friend and relative from the Rosebud Sioux Reservation and also a Sicangu Lakota. Her powerful words are found in Chapter 4, "Memories," in the book *Shaping Survival: Essays by Four American Indian Tribal Women*, edited by Jack W. Marken and Charles L. Woodard. The essays by the other three authors—Lanniko L. Lee, Florestine Kiyukanpi Renville, and Karen Lone Hill—in this necessary and significant work are no less powerful. I recommend the book highly. Thank you to Scarecrow Press of Lanham, Maryland, for permission to use Lydia's material.

Bibliography

Abourezk, James G., *The Occupation of Wounded Knee, 1973*. James G. Abourezk Papers. 1970–83.

Adams, David Wallace, *Education for Extinction—American Indians and the Boarding School Experience, 1875–1928*. University of Kansas Press. 1995.

Ambrose, Stephen A., *Undaunted Courage: Meriwether Lewis, Thomas Jefferson, and the Opening of the American West*. Simon and Schuster. 1996.

Anderson, John A., *The Sioux of the Rosebud: A History in Pictures*. University of Oklahoma. 1971.

Bergman, A., et. al., "A Political History of the Indian Health Service." *Milbank Quarterly*, Volume 77, No. 4. 1999.

Bourke, John G., *On the Border with Crook*. Time-Life Books. 1980. (Reprint)

Brown, Dee, *Fort Phil Kearny*. New York. 1962.

Buechel, Eugene, S. J., *Lakota-English Dictionary*. Red Cloud Indian School, Inc. 1970.

Buecher, Thomas R., ed., *The Crazy Horse Surrender Ledger*. Nebraska Historical Society, 1994.

Coleman, Michael, *American Indian Children at School, 1850–1930*. University of Mississippi Press. 1993.

Darling, Roger, *Custer's Seventh Cavalry Comes to Dakota: New Discoveries Reveal Custer's Tribulations Enroute to the Yellowstone Expedition*. Upton & Sons. 1988.

Deloria, Vine, Jr., *Behind the Trail of Broken Treaties*. Delacorte. 1974.

Deloria, Vine, Jr., *God is Red*. Grosset & Dunlap. 1973.

Deloria, Vine, Jr., *The World We Used to Live In: Remembering the Powers of Medicine Men*. Fulcrum Publishing. 2006.

Doll, Don, S.J., and Jim Alinder, eds., *Crying for a Vision: A Rosebud Sioux Trilogy, 1886–1976.* Morgan & Morgan. 1976.

Doyle, Susan Badger, Theodore L. Magruder, Barry Hagan, Karen White Eyes, *Civilian, Military, Native American: Portraits of Fort Phil Kearny.* Fort Phil Kearny/Bozeman Trail Association. 1993.

Field, Ron, and Adam Hook, *Forts of the American Frontier, 1820–91: Central and Northern Plains.* Osprey Publishers. 2005.

Gonzalez, Mario, Elizabeth Cook-Lynn, *The Politics of Hallowed Ground: Wound Knee and the Struggle for Indian Sovereignty.* The University of Illinois Press. 1999.

Hatch, Thom, *The Custer Companion: A Comprehensive Guide to the Life and Campaigns of George Armstrong Custer.* Stackpole Books. 2000.

Haley, James L., *The Buffalo War.* Doubleday. 1976.

Hardorff, Richard G., *The Custer Battle Casualties.* Upton & Sons. 1989.

Hardorff, Richard G., *The Custer Battle Casualties, II.* Upton & Sons. 1999.

Hedron, Paul L., *The Great Sioux War, 1876–1877.* University of Nebraska Press. 1991.

Jaimes, M. Annette, *The State of Native America—Genocide, Colonization, and Resistance.* South End Press. 1992.

LaDuke, Winona, *All Our Relations: Native Struggles for Land and Life.* South End Press. 1999.

Lazarus, Edward, *Black Hills, White Justice: The Sioux Nation Versus the United States, 1775 to the Present.* University of Nebraska Press. 1999.

Lee, Lanniko L., Florestine Kiyukanpi Renville, Karen Lone Hill, and Lydia Whirlwind Soldier, *Shaping Survival: Essays by Four American Indian Tribal Women.* Scarecrow Press. 2002.

Moulton, Gary E., ed., *The Journals of the Lewis and Clark Expedition, Volumes 1–13.* The University of Nebraska Press. 1983–2001.

Rankin, Charles E., ed., *Legacy: New Perspectives on the Battle of the Little Bighorn.* Montana Historical Society Press. 1996.

Riney, Scott, "Power and Powerlessness: The People of the Canton Asylum for Insane Indians." *South Dakota History,* Volumes 1 and 2, Spring/ Summer 1997.

Robertson, R. G., *Rotting Face: Smallpox and the American Indian.* Caxton. 2001.

Ronda, James P., *Lewis and Clark Among the Indians.* University of Nebraska Press. 2001.

Russell, Jerry, *1876 Facts about Custer and the Battle of the Little Bighorn.* Savas Publishing. 1999.

Russo, Elmer R., *A Fateful Time: The Background and Legislative History of the Indian Reorganization Act.* University of Nevada Press. 2000.

Schorr, Don, *The Ethnicity of the Seventh Cavalry,* Little Bighorn Associates Newsletter, November 2003.

Scott, Douglas D., Richard A. Fox, Jr., Melissa A. Connor, and Dick Harmon, *Archaeological Perspectives on the Battle of the Little Bighorn.* University of Oklahoma. 2000.

Tibbles, Thomas Henry, *The Ponca Chiefs.* University of Nebraska Press. 1971.

Urwin, Gregory J. W., and Ernest Lisle Reedstrom, *The United States Cavalry: An Illustrated History, 1776–1944.* Red River Books. 2003.

Walter, John, *The Guns that Won the West—Firearms on the American Frontier, 1848–1898.* Greenhill Books. 1999.

Washburn, Wilcomb E., *The Assault on Indian Tribalism: The General Allotment Law (Dawes Act of 1887).* Krieger Publishing Company. 1986. (Reprint)

White Hat, Albert, Sr., *Reading and Writing the Lakota Language.* University of Utah Press. 1999.

Witmer, Linda F., *The Indian Industrial School, Carlisle, Pennsylvania, 1879–1918.* Cumberland County Historical Society. 1993.

Veterans Affairs Committee of the United States Senate, *Medal Of Honor, 1863–1978, "in the name of the Congress of the United States."* Ameron, Ltd. 1996.

Government Records

1876 Monthly Returns, Seventh U.S. Cavalry. National Archives.

1876 Muster Rolls, Seventh U.S. Cavalry. National Archives.

Bureau of American Ethnology, *The Ghost Dance Religion and the Sioux Outbreak of 1890,* 14th Annual Report (1892–93), Part 2. Smithsonian Institute, Washington, D.C. 1895.

McLaughlin, James, Report to the Office of Indian Affairs, #39602, *Account of the Death of Sitting Bull and of the Circumstances Attending It.* Philadelphia, 1891.

State of South Dakota, Department of Corrections. Adult Monthly Statistics. Adult Inmates by Race, August 1, 2006.

South Dakota State Library, *Canton Asylum Annual Reports (1903–1933).* Microfilm Reels.

United States Senate Committee on the Judiciary, *Wounded Knee Massacre.* U.S. Government Printing Office. 1976.

United States Department of Commerce, *Federal and Indian State Reservations and Indian Trust Areas.* U.S. Government Printing Office. 1974.

United States Department of the Interior, Bureau of Indian Affairs, Canton Asylum, 1921–24. *Indian Census Rolls, 1885–1940.* National Archives Microfilm Publications.

United States Department of the Interior, Bureau of Indian Affairs, *Treaty of Fort Laramie, September 17, 1851.* U.S. Government Printing Office.

United States Department of the Interior, Bureau of Indian Affairs, *Fort Laramie Treaty, April 29, 1868. Treaty with the Sioux—Brule, Oglala, Miniconjou, Yanktonai, Hunkpapa, Blackfeet, Cuthead, Two Kettle, Sans Arcs, and Santee—and Arapaho.* U.S. Government Printing Office.

United States Department of the Interior, Bureau of Indian Affairs Indian Relocation Records. Cheyenne River Agency; Pierre Agency; Sisseton Agency.

Index

Page numbers in *italics* indicate
maps.

For more from Joseph M. Marshall III, look for the

The Journey of Crazy Horse
A Lakota History
As the peerless warrior who brought the U.S. Army to its knees at
the Battle of Little Bighorn, Crazy Horse remains one of the most
perennially fascinating figures of the American West. Now Joseph
Marshall goes beyond that, drawing on extensive research and a rich
oral tradition that is rarely shared outside the Native American community. He gives us a riveting portrait of Crazy Horse, from the
powerful vision that spurred him into battle to the woman he loved
but lost to circumstance. *The Journey of Crazy Horse* celebrates a
long-standing community's enduring culture and gives vibrant life to
its most trusted and revered hero.

ISBN 978-0-14-303621-0

The Lakota Way
Stories and Lessons for Living
Rich with storytelling, history, and folklore, *The Lakota Way* ex-
presses the heart of Native American philosophy and imparts the
path to a fulfilling and meaningful life. Joseph Marshall is a member
of the Sicunga Lakota Sioux and has dedicated his entire life to the
wisdom he learned from his elders. Here he focuses on the twelve
core qualities that are crucial to the Lakota way of living—bravery,
fortitude, generosity, wisdom, respect, honor, perseverance, love, humility, sacrifice, truth, and compassion. Whether teaching a lesson on
respect imparted by the mythical Deer Woman or the humility embodied by the legendary Lakota leader Crazy Horse, *The Lakota
Way* offers a fresh outlook on spirituality and ethical living.

ISBN 978-0-14-219609-0